MW01052018

"Susan Piedmont-Palladino provides wonderful insight into the various types and functions of drawings. This valuable book is both practical and inspirational and should be read by architects as well as students of design and others interested in built environments."

Frederick Steiner, Dean, School of Design, University of Pennsylvania

"No need to be an architect to appreciate this erudite, illustrated exploration of communication through drawing. Susan Piedmont-Palladino critically analyzes drawing types, purposes, pitfalls and history, from cave art to digital modeling. Yet her insightful, intellectually rigorous writing, often punctuated with 'just-between-you-and-me' asides, is witty and charmingly conversational."

Roger K. Lewis, FAIA, Architect & Planner, Professor Emeritus,
University of Maryland School of Architecture, Planning and
Preservation, Columnist, The Washington Post

"Susan Piedmont-Palladino has written a book about drawing unlike any other. She recounts her own discovery of the depth and diversity of architectural drawings, exploring analogies with language and finding parallels with art history. It is an accessible book and a deeply personal and philosophical one as well, and it is well worth the time it takes to read."

Professor Thomas Fisher, Director of the Minnesota Design
Center at the University of Minnesota

"Piedmont-Palladino takes you on an unexpected journey into a world of groundbreaking scholarship illuminated with startling 'aha' moments and profoundly witty observations. She makes you think and she makes you laugh—sometimes sequentially, sometimes simultaneously. If you have ever seen a drawing or made a drawing, you will want to read this book. Now that I have read it, how I think about language and about drawing will never be the same again."

Chase W. Rynd, Executive Director and CEO,
National Building Museum

"*How Drawings Work* is an altogether marvelous contribution to the literature on representation. Moving with agility across a range of perspectives—aesthetic philosophy and linguistic theory, architectural history and professional practice, science fiction and commercial advertising—Susan Piedmont-Palladino crafts a series of insightful arguments on the changing nature of architectural communication."

Nancy Levinson, Places Journal

"Piedmont-Palladino understands how architects' use tools not just to design but find our way through the world. This wise exploration expands our understanding of how and why architects communicate—to each other and those who inhabit our creations—and deftly challenges the false choice between the analog and the digital by reframing our understanding of both."

Phil Bernstein, Associate Dean and Senior Lecturer, Yale School of
Architecture and former Vice President at Autodesk

"Susan Piedmont-Palladino's boundless imagination shines in her new book. With grace and wit, she reveals the intellectually rich history of the architect's most basic tool—the drawing. Utterly delightful."

Lance Hosey, author of The Shape of Green: Aesthetics, Ecology, and Design

HOW DRAWINGS WORK

How Drawings Work cheekily explains that what architects make is information that enables other people to make buildings. That information comes in a variety of forms: drawings by hand and computer, models both physical and virtual, and words as needed. The book reflects in witty prose on the nature of architectural drawings as tools of communication, pulling from a diverse and eclectic landscape of theories from grammar, functional linguistics, philosophy, art criticism, science fiction, popular culture, and, of course, architecture, to propose a new way to think about architectural communication.

Susan C. Piedmont-Palladino is a professor of Architecture, Coordinator of Urban Design, and the Director of Virginia Tech's Washington / Alexandria Architecture Center in Alexandria, Virginia, USA. She is also a curator at the National Building Museum in Washington, District of Columbia, and a registered architect in the Commonwealth of Virginia, USA.

HOW DRAWINGS WORK

A USER-FRIENDLY THEORY

SUSAN C. PIEDMONT-PALLADINO

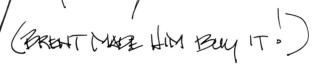

(BRENT MADE HIM BUY IT!)

Routledge
Taylor & Francis Group

NEW YORK AND LONDON

First published 2019
by Routledge
52 Vanderbilt Avenue, New York, NY 10017

and by Routledge
2 Park Square, Milton Park, Abingdon, Oxon, OX14 4RN

Routledge is an imprint of the Taylor & Francis Group, an informa business

© 2019 Taylor & Francis

The right of Susan C. Piedmont-Palladino to be identified as author of this
work has been asserted by her in accordance with sections 77 and 78 of the
Copyright, Designs and Patents Act 1988.

All rights reserved. No part of this book may be reprinted or reproduced or
utilized in any form or by any electronic, mechanical, or other means, now
known or hereafter invented, including photocopying and recording, or in
any information storage or retrieval system, without permission in writing
from the publishers.

Trademark notice: Product or corporate names may be trademarks or
registered trademarks, and are used only for identification and explanation
without intent to infringe.

Library of Congress Cataloging-in-Publication Data
Names: Piedmont-Palladino, Susan, author.
Title: How drawings work : a user-friendly theory / Susan C.
    Piedmont-Palladino.
Description: New York : Routledge, 2019. | Includes bibliographical
    references and index.
Identifiers: LCCN 2018034976 | ISBN 9781138692961 (hb : alk. paper) |
    ISBN 9781138692978 (pb : alk. paper) | ISBN 9781315531410 (ebook)
Subjects: LCSH: Architectural drawing.
Classification: LCC NA2700 .P53 2019 | DDC 720.28/4—dc23
LC record available at https://lccn.loc.gov/2018034976

ISBN: 978-1-138-69296-1 (hbk)
ISBN: 978-1-138-69297-8 (pbk)
ISBN: 978-1-315-53141-0 (ebk)

Typeset in Univers LT Std
by Apex CoVantage, LLC

Printed in Canada

Dorathy Brown Piedmont 1927–2014

CONTENTS

ACKNOWLEDGMENTS

Writing a book is not only an autographic experience, as Nelson Goodman would put it, it is also a lonely one. We run our ideas by our colleagues seeking validation, test them on students in search of evidence, bore friends with our theories hoping for encouragement, but ultimately it is I, the author, alone with the keyboard, the page, and a pressing urgency to speak. One voice in my head says "go ahead, this is great stuff, truly original!" while the other says, "you have no idea what you're talking about." That is when I relied on my colleagues, students, and friends for comments, questions, and suggestions. What follow is as comprehensive a list as I can make of all those who helped me get here.

I owe a profound thanks to the two institutions that have both shaped my perspective on the built world and given me the intellectual space to investigate my myriad questions about it: Virginia Tech and the National Building Museum. Virginia Tech has provided me a home at the Washington Alexandria Architecture Center, known to all as the WAAC, where I have taught for most of my career. There I am surrounded by creative colleagues and the best students in the world. My students, named and unnamed, have been an inexhaustible source of reflection, surprise, and amusement. Even though I have used some student work to illustrate quirky or odd drawings, the work they do is undertaken with sincerity. Among the joys of teaching is getting to see things you have never seen before, and hearing thoughts you have never thought before.

It was a question I posed to my late colleague Marco Frascari that started this entire inquiry: did he have any suggestion, I asked, for anything I could read on the idea of the subjunctive in drawing? If anyone knew, I figured, he would. Instead of giving me a list of obscure texts, he said: I don't know of any such thing; I think you should write it. As I plowed ahead, Paola Frascari, Marco's wife and a master of languages, generously shared her thoughts on grammar. All my faculty colleagues at the WAAC especially the incomparable Jaan Holt—my predecessor as Director—have continued to encourage me even as this has dragged on longer than it should have. I have relied on the serious scholarship of others, like colleague Paul Emmons, and eagerly pounced on book recommendations from others. I never would have known about Arthur Stinchcombe were it not for Matt Dull.

I also want to thank my colleagues in the English Department at Virginia Tech, especially Jane Wemhoener, for her initial enthusiasm, when I shared this topic so many years ago in the garden of the Steger Center in Riva San Vitale, and her continued encouragement. Also professors Katie Powell, Joe Scallorns, and their son Henry, whose innocent insight warranted a note in Chapter 2. I am grateful for the cheerful assistance of two graduate assistants at the WAAC who helped me with original graphics and the tedious task of scanning and rescanning images: Marium Rahman and Alyssa Tope.

The start of my work as a writer and curator with the National Building Museum coincided with the beginnings of this writing, so I can both thank—and blame—the Museum: the thanks are for giving me the precious opportunity to communicate complex issues to an interested public; the blame for all the wonderful exhibitions and books I curated and wrote that distracted me from finishing this project. My experience as a curator and writer gave me the opportunity to develop a voice to speak to an interested public, an audience that is quite different from an academic one. I am profoundly grateful to the Museum's Executive Director Chase Rynd and Vice President for Exhibitions and Collections Cathy Frankel for patiently accepting my odd work schedule.

A special thanks goes to the National Gallery of Art in Washington, D.C., particularly to archivist Michelle Willens who first guided me through her collection years ago when I was on a sabbatical trying to figure out how to put these ideas into a coherent form. When I emailed years later to confess that I had not finished anything, we picked up where we left off. Michelle tipped me off to the curious division of the drawings, between the Archives and the Modern Prints and Drawings Collection. Carlotta Owens, who presided over the latter collection, was also a gracious help. The National Gallery was and is a treasure, a wonderful place to spend parts of my days, bent over huge tables looking at original drawings.

Thanks are due to the unnamed design professionals and clients who unwittingly provided me with such great anecdotal material and to those who have shared their own design process comedies of errors in conversations, reassuring me that my tales are not outliers. At the precarious point in the writing process when near-completion summoned a bad case of doubt, Nancy Levinson and her editorial team at *PLACES Journal*, welcomed a ratty draft and then published an excerpt, Chapter 7. The response was a well-timed clap of validation to see me through to the end.

I save my heaviest heap of thanks for my patient and devoted husband, Douglas Palladino, who read, questioned, suggested, image-searched—and created—encouraged, and nudged me particularly when this research became so much background static after a few publisher rejections. As my mantra "when I finish my book" became "when I finish my d**n book," I became even more selfish about my time yet he never wavered in his support for this.

PREFACE

It's been said that Americans and the British are two peoples separated by a common language[1], and the same could be said for artists and architects. To the outside observer we seem to be first cousins, allies in the creation and production of the visual and physical world. Moreover, our works are equally subject to aesthetic judgment. But things are not at all that simple. Anyone who has come to architecture from a background in fine arts probably remembers the pain of unlearning certain ways of seeing, drawing, and assembling things. Former art majors may have been puzzled, as I was, that my undergraduate degree in the history of art, which had seemed to be ideal preparation for a graduate degree in architecture, did not in fact put me ahead of my peers from literature, computer science, and management. Apparently, I didn't even draw correctly. I quickly learned that the feathery strokes I had mastered were best left for the eyebrow pencil. Caffeine, sugar, and fear quickly gave my sketches the architect's sanctioned wiggly line. Only my grounding in history and theory—the slide file of knowledge in my head—was a clear advantage and even then only during the lightning round.

My liberal and fine arts roots did prove useful in architectural practice, just not quite in the way that I expected, and that background has proven essential for me as an educator, which is now my primary profession. Although architecture remains my field of inquiry, what I actually do as an educator is quite different from what I did as an architect. I talk for a living. And listen. The fundamental delivery system of architectural education is the design studio, which is a labor-intensive, space-consuming, and intimate learning environment. The individual student is the center of this universe. I visit students at their desks, in their own space, to sit by their side and listen to their struggles and aspirations. Then I have to figure out what to say to help them develop into the kind of design professional they want to be. It would be easy to pick up a pencil and draw a solution for them, but that's not the way—at least, that's not my way—to teach design. So, I have to craft a way to talk to each student about his or her individual projects and problems.

One year I had a student who was exceptionally thoughtful and imaginative but he inhabited his own world graphically. He had invented his own drawing conventions; he had his own codes and marks that meant something only to him. Near the end the semester I was nudging, cajoling, and encouraging him to draw the project in such a way that we—his professors—could see it as a real architectural proposal. "You want me to do working drawings?" he asked, referring to the detailed and dimensioned drawings that architects prepare for builders. No,

I answered. First, I explained, it doesn't matter what *I* want, (this is my usual parry when a student asks if I like something, or tries to give me what he thinks I want). What matters, I explained, is your fulfillment of the promise of your architectural idea, that you make it as realized as possible...even though we both know it isn't real. Think of your building like a novel, a work of fiction, I told him. It needs to be internally consistent and internally real. Its reality just doesn't happen to coincide with ours. Draw it as if it's real, as if you have seen it and you're drawing to remember having seen it. Learning to draw "working drawings" is certainly important, but not here and not now; they have a very different audience.

As I explained this to him, it dawned on me that I was using a particular mode of language to get my point across: the subjunctive, which is the language of wishes, desires, and conditions contrary to fact. This is the language of "as if." Maybe, I began to wonder, the subjunctive was the language of design drawings themselves. If so, are there indicative and imperative drawings as well, these being the big three verb modes? Thus a research agenda was born: if, like verb modes, drawings establish certain relations to the world, then a close look at drawings will reveal marks, techniques, and inflections that both describe and make that world.

I came to architecture from the liberal arts and I brought with me a long-standing fascination with language, which may in part explain why I would ruminate on how the subjunctive applies to graphics. For this I blame my high school Latin teacher, the late and feared[2] Mr. Carr. He said something once that has stuck with me all these years. To be honest, he said many things that stuck with me. I remember a great deal from my four years of Latin at Glen Ridge High School, not the least of which is how to decline Coca Cola and a piece of cake ("no thank you" is the correct answer to the latter; Junior Classical Leaguers will know the answer to the former). I can also recite from memory the first seven lines of the *Aeneid* and, if pressed, determine the day's Latin date. Mr. Carr scared this stuff straight into my brain, a teaching method I completely disavow as an educator myself but which, I grudgingly have to admit, worked on me at the time. These memories are entertaining empathy generators in the unlikely event that I meet someone who also studied Latin in high school, but they are more than that. Mr. Carr said one thing, almost in passing, to our tiny combined Latin III-IV class, that was profound. He said that the subjunctive mode is what made poetry possible.

Why would I remember such a comment? I, along with my five or six classmates, was struggling mightily with the rhetorical conventions of Virgil—zeugma, anyone?—as well as with the seemingly infinite possible endings for verbs as they shape-shifted their modes, tenses, and voices. The subjunctive was the most confounding, so perhaps Mr. Carr was trying to get us to appreciate the effort, to understand that it was all worth something in the end. It was worth poetry. I don't think I had ever thought that some *thing*, like a grammatical invention, was responsible for the existence of poetry. I accepted that poetry, like everything else in the world, simply *was*. Teens accept the inevitability of the world, boring and embarrassing, as it is. For some reason this thought about poetry stayed with me, though, and that is how I came to love the subjunctive.

While the indicative mode let us name and describe the world, and the imperative empowered us to make others do something about it, the subjunctive released our imagination and allowed the representation of the possible. It let us wonder how the world might be different if... if we were to *imagine*. That word itself is already sitting right in the middle of the visual world and built directly on the Latin noun for "picture" and on the reflexive verb "to picture oneself." Imagination is our capacity to picture something in our minds, whether or not it is present or even real, whether it is a memory or a fabrication. Without the subjunctive, there is no imagination. Put another way, in the subjunctive: *were* it not for the subjunctive, there would be no imagination...in language or in architecture.

As an educator, I search for a language to use with students that isn't a degraded or pretend form of client/architect language; nor a subjective language of taste and preference; nor simply a litany of assignments and prescriptions without explanation. As an educator, I need a language that recognizes that a student's design drawings differ *fundamentally*, in kind not just in scope, from those done in practice. A student project constitutes a fully conceived architectural thought, but, except in rare circumstances, it is one that will live always and only in the parallel universe of the imagination. It remains a wish contrary to fact, and this has representational implications for *all* design drawings, for the built, the unbuilt, and the unlikely-to-be-built, and the never-gonna-be-built, the last categories being where student work and theoretical or unlucky professional work intersects. How to convey that situation, how to ask for this line and not that, for a sheet organized thus, a model made of this—these questions have led me here to this wrestling match with several contentious conversations in architecture and architectural education today: what do the rules of natural language offer the study of graphic language? Why is communication between architects and their publics so fraught? Why the crevasse between intentions and interpretations? What are our drawings saying? Do hand drawings and digital drawings speak in the same language? How do drawings make a world? How do they continue to work—because they do—even after the building is built?

It may seem at first that I'm revisiting the much plowed field of "architecture as language," just one of our profession's serial attempts to understand architect "as" something else that appears to be more understandable. As you will see—if you keep reading—I'm taking a slightly different path through the linguistic forest, using the concept of mode or mood in language as an analogy to illuminate architectural drawing. It may be, as I develop this argument and then see what others can do with it, that at some point we might leave the analogy behind and seize the terminology for our own purposes, kicking the crutch of extra-architectural support from beneath us so we can limp along on our own. We will have abducted new names for ways of drawing.

This book was originally intended to be a dense academic tome, which would begin with a review of literature on the subject—surely someone else had

had this idea—followed by close readings of various examples of drawings, until I had proven my point that architectural drawings can be categorized by modes analogous to the verb modes of natural language: the indicative, subjunctive, and imperative. It was all going to be very dissertation-ish. In the far too many years since I began this project, though, the language has loosened and the subject matter expanded, even as the verb mode trinity remains the core. This research and rambling remains rooted in my teaching but in recent years has been enriched by my work as a museum curator where I translate the language of architecture into something an interested public can understand.

This became a much more personal project after my mother died in 2014 because she is the one who taught me to draw. She was an artist who drew gracefully and faithfully from life—portraits, still lives, figures. She would set a pitcher and bowl of fruit on the kitchen table for me to draw after school while she cooked. She would correct my line work, proportions, and shadows. After she died I became the keeper of all of her drawings, dating back to when she was a child. Her mother had kept hers, and I discovered that she had in turn kept all of mine. I have now a remarkable collection of what each of us drew at the same ages, thirty years apart. Hers are consistently better than mine are (see Figures 0.1 and 0.2). As I grew up and turned toward architecture, I began to draw

FIGURE 0.1   At about seven years old I drew the family living room, so detailed that I can recognize the furniture and objects on the mantle.

FIGURE 0.2 My mother, Dorathy Brown Piedmont, drew her grandmother's living room when she was eleven. Her mother helpfully dated the back of the drawing.

differently. When I was a child, I drew from the world, as my mother taught me; when I became an architect, I drew toward it. My reflections on that paradigmatic shift are the foundation of this book.

NOTES

1. Churchill? George Bernard Shaw? Between them, they've said most everything.
2. This phrase, "late and feared" is an example of the rhetorical figure known as hysteron-proteron. Mr. Carr described it as putting the cart before the horse, putting two terms in an order the reverse of what they represent in time. Using this figure pays homage to Mr. Carr, feared before his demise.

CHAPTER 1
INTRODUCTION: AN IRRESPONSIBLY BRIEF HISTORY OF DRAWING(S)

Talking does not make the world or even pictures, but talking and pictures participate in making each other and the world as we know them.

Nelson Goodman, *Languages of Art*

LET'S JUST START AT THE BEGINNING: it turns out, there really are two bison. And, it turns out that the particular lens you bring to a problem determines what you see; different disciplines see the same things differently. An art historian looking at ancient cave paintings looks for those things that art historians look for: regional variations, inventiveness, and evolution of style and skill over time, as if the cave painters had worked their way through the archaic, classical, and mannerist phases of cave painting. The art historian would attend closely to these things in search of a key to unlock the meaning of a drawing. This can pose a challenge with pre-historic images. With no written record to explain the origin or purpose of the drawings, we have only the mute evidence of lines, colors, and marks to interpret. Historians love paper trails; they trust them. A historian working without a text is unmoored. So, with no graphic equivalent to the Rosetta Stone to crack open their meaning, the cave paintings of Lascaux or Pergouset have obsessed us—art historians and lay persons alike—because they are loaded with visual eloquence and verbal *praecisio*. Instead of written records, we have nothing but our long culturally constructed history of image-making and attendant commentary to guide our interpretation.

When we see an image of a bison, drawn with the economy of line and gesture that our modern eyes have learned to value, we have no contemporaneous text to which we can refer. What was the purpose of this drawing? What was it supposed to do? Was this, we wonder, a documentation of an actual bison, intended to be as realistic a portrait of the painter's favorite bison? Maybe it was a depiction of a past bison who met an unfortunate fate, the pre-historic equivalent of Instagramming your food. It could have been a warning to other humans not to come too close to this cave because a bison such as this might be lurking inside.[1] Is it the expression of a desire, an invocation, for a bison to enter into the painter's life that day? Perhaps it is rhetorical, intended to persuade early peoples to act or not. Perhaps it's the work of a Cro-Magnon Magritte: *ce n'est pas un taureau!* And all the witty primitives would nod in appreciation of such cleverness.

The art historian muses over these images and interprets the graphic variations in the context of what he has deemed to be the drawing's purpose. Consider these two drawings of bison (see Figure 1.1): Bison A was drawn on the walls of the caves in Lascaux. It presents long curved horns that look intimidating and a slightly swept-back posture that suggests he could be ready to charge. This drawing must be a warning. Bison B was drawn in a cave in Pergouset. This one seems docile; standing upright with eyes downcast, he shows no sign of impending movement. He looks like a good target for hunters; his horns are nothing to fear. From this description one could construct an interpretation that the painters of Lascaux lived in fear of their bison; those of Pergouset, on the other hand, were master hunters who, yes, Instagrammed their food. Supporting this interpretation is evidence that the Pergouset bison is a later drawing, by about three thousand years.[2] Under this interpretive regime, we might use that paleontological fact to propose that by then our ancient selves had begun to dominate the bison with new and better tools, and so of course the representations would reflect that. Now look back at the two bison drawings: supplemented by this narrative their graphic differences appear to be logically consistent with this altered perception of our relation to each subject. One bison, two different human perceptions.

When a paleontologist looks at the same images, she probably agrees with the art historian, but for very different reasons. She knows that there's no fossil record of Bison B during the Pleistocene; ergo, it couldn't have existed. Bison A, yes, that's a *real* bison. The fossil record tells us so. Bison B? No evidence, no bison. Bison B was clearly a product of early human imagination, a fiction. We now have an interpretation of these two images supported by data from two very different fields. Together art and paleontology have established a mutually reinforcing reality: bison that looked like Bison A existed, but no bison that looked like Bison B existed. The differences in the two mammals' appearance then are due to different artistic intentions or stylistic developments. The great swoop of horns in Bison A versus the meager wiggles of B's don't represent different environmental adaptations in evolving species, they represent more confident line work.[3]

a

Steppe bison-like morphology

b

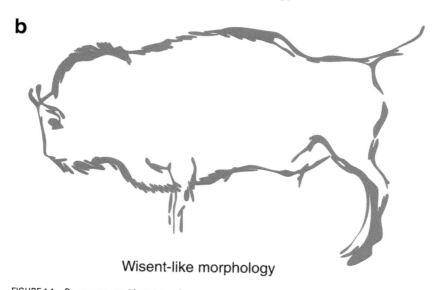

Wisent-like morphology

FIGURE 1.1   Do you see one bison or two?

Then the geneticist shows up. He's curious about Bison B, because he notices that it looks a lot like a known bison, the European bison, or wisent (*Bison bonasus*), which "has no recognized Pleistocene fossil record and seems to suddenly appear in the early Holocene."[4] One need not be a geneticist to know that bison don't magically materialize; just because there is an absence of fossil evidence of the bison's existence doesn't mean it didn't exist. Nothing doesn't prove anything. So the geneticist did the sort of exhaustive tests that geneticists do and concluded: "The coincident morphological and genetic replacement indicate that variation in bison representations in Paleolithic art does not simply represent stylistic evolution, but actually reflects the different forms of bison genotyped in the study (that is, pre- and post-hybridization) through time."[5] In other words, there was a Bison B. It wasn't an evolution of drawings styles; it was a Darwinian evolution of the actual bison.

How do these bison drawings work? They testify; they document. Even the most ancient ones remain alive and useful, not only as portals into understanding our own deep past but, as we now know, to illuminate the lives of other species. The cave painters have been speaking to us all this time, saying, "I drew what I saw accurately; my drawing is evidence that this particular bison existed. Are you going to believe the fossil record, or are you going to believe me? I drew this thing you call the wisent. My drawing is the evidence of its existence" (see Figure 1.2). Every drawing, every representation, everything that we make establishes a relation to the world. The question facing anyone who makes a drawing is: exactly what relation with the world do you intend to establish with this drawing? What do you intend this drawing to do? We can call these bison images evidence now because they are behaving as such for us, but they were probably doing some other work in their time. Bison happen to be a favorite subject of the most ancient human drawings; there are 820 known "depictions displaying bison individuals (~21% of known cave ornamentation)."[6] There must have been a reason for their quantitative dominance. We moderns tend to see these drawings as art, ascribing creative intention to them and evaluating their mastery, but this new extra-graphical information lets us see them differently. In that sense, we risk reducing the drawings' relations to the world by seeing them only as factual depictions and congratulating ourselves for having solved a scientific mystery.

Other mysteries, however, remain and there are other possible relations to the world established by the drawings of the bison. Our ancestors perhaps drew these figures on the walls out of fear, longing, or to summon magical powers. They could be incantations, prayers for a favorable hunt. They could have served as talismans, to ward off something. In that case, they establish what we might call, borrowing from grammar, a *volitional* or *optative* relation to the world, an urgent and active wish for an outcome. Optative expressions are pleas, prayers, exhortations, and wishes, and they are a class of the subjunctive, which is the verb mode capable of describing a range of such uncertainties. An optative drawing of a bison says, "may we have a successful hunt tomorrow." Whether they were drawn accurately to depict the local livestock or graphically to urge the gods to favor our hunt, the purpose of these ancient drawings will never be resolved, but we can be confident of one thing: they were *not* instructions on how to *make* a bison. These very different functions of drawings are the subject of this book.

LOOSE PARTS

FIGURE 1.2 Cartoonist Dave Blazek explains the origins and purpose of cave drawings.

The cave paintings in Lascaux weren't discovered until 1940, so we first saw them through modern eyes—eyes that had already seen Michelangelo, Picasso, and Matisse. These eyes were primed to appreciate certain aspects of the cave paintings *qua* paintings, not only as documentations or as exhortations potentially saturated with meaning. By this point in the twentieth century, we had learned to separate form and meaning, thanks to shifts in artistic intentions and interpretations.[7] With the discovery of these ancient paintings, we finally had some hard evidence for the origin of drawing, but we have been puzzling over its purpose ever since.

Not having had the same benefit of seeing these cave paintings, ancient writers had to invent their own origin myths for drawing and painting. Pliny the Elder's myth of the origin of drawing is one of the most referenced in literature about the making of art. Writing his *Natural History* in the first century CE, he first says that the origins of painting are uncertain, and irrelevant to the book he's writing. In a bit of Roman braggadocio, he is dismissive of the Egyptians' claim "that it was invented among themselves six thousand years ago"[8] and then they shared it with the Greeks. Whomever deserves the credit, all agree, he says, "it began with tracing an outline round a man's shadow."[9] He then recounts the romantic story of young Butades, tracing the candlelight-cast shadow of her departing lover on the wall so that she may remember him while he is gone.[10]

What we know about the vast archive of images from history comes from the stories that have accompanied them, the captions that cling to them, or the web of correspondence, receipts, and inventories that form the basis of art history scholarship. Text and image have a long and difficult partnership. When text enters the cave, so to speak, it changes how we see the bison. We know the bison only through the mute image, unaccompanied, at least originally, by textual interpretation. We know Butades's drawing solely through texts; the accompanying image appears only in our minds, or in the various interpretations of artists inspired to depict it.

Jan Van Eyck's *Portrait of Arnolfini and His Wife* is both an interesting image and an interesting story—or set of multiple stories—which has kept art historians busy for years. Here we get both image and text, pictures and words. The title itself shapes our understanding of it; alternate titles, such as *Portrait of Arnolfini and Her Lover*, or *Rendering of Proposed Master Bedroom*, would make us look at it completely differently. The words direct our attention to certain things and blind us to others, thus the copious ink spilled about the mirror, where all sorts of subject matter hides in plain yet uncaptioned sight. What relationship to the world is Van Eyck establishing with this image? That Arnolfini and his wife existed and they looked something like this? Is the title sufficient evidence for us to accept his image as documentation? We don't need genetics or a fossil record in this case, but we still want some assurance that claims made in the text are validated in the image, and vice versa. It is of course not quite that simple, which philosopher Nelson Goodman makes clear in *Languages of Art*, his fascinating and comprehensive little book on image-making. According to Goodman, we really have no way of knowing whether this is a "realistic" portrait of the happy couple, as we are in no position to make a point-to-point comparison from human to painting. As Goodman explains, though, we don't really require that kind of proof in this circumstance, as "the touchstone of realism" is not in the "quantity of information but in how easily it issues. And this depends upon how stereotyped the mode of representation is, upon how commonplace the labels and their uses have become"[11] In other words, there is a way of representing certain kinds of people, known as a "portrait," and furthermore, labeling the representation with the subjects' names provides a solid touchstone. How does this painting work?[12] Its purpose is to *show* us, with high probability of correspondence, Arnolfini and his wife. It is not to offer suggestions for the design and furnishing of a room.

Another familiar "stereotyped mode of representation" is the "artist's rendering," that staple of mass media that helps illustrate something that is impossible to see, can no longer be seen, or cannot yet be seen. For example, *National Geographic* might show a Neanderthal family (cave painting bison specialists?), *Popular Science* might illustrate a cut-away of the sun, or *Scientific American* might offer images of colorful exoplanets. What exactly are these images and how are they supposed to work? Who is this "artist" and where or when is she standing that things look this way? *Popular Science* published a story in 2011 on the discovery of arsenic-loving microbes at Mono Lake that showed promise as possible models for extra-terrestrial life forms. The geobiochemist/astrobiologist who made the discovery was concerned that the NASA-produced explanatory video left misleading impressions, thereby blurring the boundary between science and speculation. "It clearly says 'artist's interpretation,' but maybe that doesn't work for biology. With astronomy, people seem to be comfortable looking at cartoons and not holding scientists accountable for those purple planets. But with biology, it's looked at as data."[13] For her—and biologists—the images are as beholden to evidence as the science itself. The image "speaks" with the same authority as the data, and therefore context matters, as does the tone of "voice." The purple planet people have an entirely different problem apparently.

Scientific American, aware of the misplaced comfort of its readers "looking at cartoons" of exoplanets on its pages, published an article with the wonderfully obvious title "How Do Artists Portray Exoplanets They've Never Seen?" In it, the magazine shared its struggles for a careful balance between artist's imagination and scientific evidence, and how to make clear which is which.[14] One of the magazine's artists, Lynette Cook, was surprised when she received an email from a reader who thought that one of her paintings—done for the scientific press release on the discovery of planet HD209458 in 1999 (see Figure 1.3)—was an actual photograph, and wanted to know what image processing software she had used to produce it: "A lot of people didn't understand that it was a rendering."[15] That kind of realism may be a source of pride for the artist—is it live or is it Memorex?—but it can be a concern for scientists. Researcher Felice Frankel worried that these vivid renderings of exoplanets convey to readers a certainty about the situation that is out of proportion to the scientific knowledge. "The more, quote, 'real' something looks, the more you accept it as fact."[16] Thanks to our new powerful digital tools, that is increasingly a dilemma posed by hyperreal architectural renderings, which is the subject of Chapter 7.

FIGURE 1.3   Artist Lynette Cook's speculative rendering of planet HD209458.

The problem arises most acutely in images where the subject depicted cannot be proven *not* to exist, like a plausibly glowing exoplanet or a possible building wedged into a real context, or even that bison. That is an awkward way to describe what we might call the centaur problem, following Nelson Goodman: "… for even though there are no centaurs, a realistic picture might deceive me into taking it for a centaur."[17] When an image has no verifiable "compliant"—Goodman's term for the thing outside of the work to which the work refers or intends—how is a viewer to assess whether it is "realistic?" In the case of the bison, the assessment of its reality, its verification, came from another field, genetics. The realism of the Arnolfinis' portrait depends on the title and on our trust as viewers that the correspondence between word and image is valid. But as far as any reader of *Scientific America* is concerned, that is what an exoplanet looks like. Just try to prove otherwise. Somewhere between intention and interpretation, all sorts of mischief can happen.

What do cave paintings, Flemish portraits, and speculative renderings of exoplanets all have in common? They all rely on evidence that is in the world; they literally draw from the world. The cave paintings, we now know, depict actual bison that shared the earth with their painters; someone saw them and drew what they saw. Arnolfini and his wife could gaze at their finished portrait and nod or frown about their appearance, but no one could deny that the painting was "of" the Arnolfinis. Even the exoplanets, which no one has seen—and as such, they are not at all like the bison—rest on a base of scientific evidence: colors signify chemical composition; size and mass are deduced from observations. The renderings are "of" the hypothetical exoplanets. These drawings work to show something that we can reasonably assume exists or did exist at some point; they depict stuff in the world. That, however, is not how all drawings work. There are drawings that work very differently and establish an entirely different relation to the world. The purpose of those drawings is to act on the world rather than document it, and it is important to know which is which. Designers—a category of imaginative world-makers that includes but is not limited to architects—make drawings and representations, the goal of which is to wish or instruct a new thing into existence. They draw *toward* the world.

Drawings establish a relationship to the world. Just like language, they can whisper and shout, contradict their authors, make promises, describe, denote, and instruct. The following chapters will explore the work that drawings do and how they do it, but here we have to explain why this is important. A lot is at stake. We are surrounded by buildings and places, almost all of which at some point existed in a flattened state on paper or screen. Even the most private construction project—an addition in the back of a house or a cabin in remote woods—is in someone else's way, leveraging capital, consuming resources, changing views, casting a new shadow, diverting water, and changing habitats. In that sense, there is no "private" architecture; all building draws from the commons. Because of that, people expect—and deserve—to be consulted when their lives are being changed by a project they didn't ask for. Thus we see the increasingly obligatory ritual of the "public presentation." At their worst, these presentations involve architects and developers presenting a *fait accompli*, pretending to listen to members of the public who are in turn pretending to listen to the architect. Few are truly listening. Instead, they are *looking*[18]...looking at floor plans that reduce the known world to lines, at sections that look like buildings peeled open by disaster (see Figure 1.4), at elevations that look like building faces pressed against glass, and, most of all, at those suspiciously seductive perspectives.

An authentically productive public meeting, one that is an exchange of concerns and assurances, is unlikely when the parties involved are communicating in different languages, and that is exactly what happens when an architect presents a project to a room of citizens. The public communicates in words; the architect, in drawings. Unfortunately, for this public process, there are probably few people in the audience who are fluent in the language of drawing, and there may be few or none on a design review committee, which may, on the basis of drawings, have the power to alter or halt a project. To be fair, there are design review boards, such as the Commission on Fine Arts in Washington, D.C. and State Historical Preservation Review Boards, that reserve a certain number of seats for design professionals, but most local boards and homeowner associations are composed of motivated volunteers rather than design professionals. In fact, zoning and design review boards rarely demand that all members exhibit

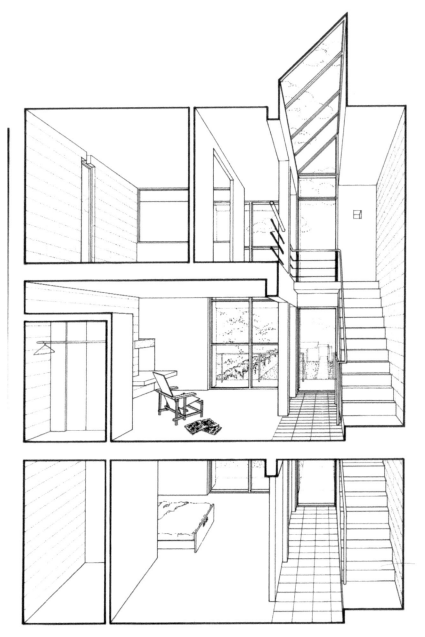

FIGURE 1.4   A section perspective is like a view into a dollhouse with its front wall removed. The occupants, surprised at the exposure, have walked out, leaving the newspaper on the floor.

fluency in the language of drawing.[19] Thus motivation, not qualification, tends to set the agenda. If a neighborhood establishes a design review protocol out of fear of, or in reaction to, a despised project, then obstruction is the motivation and thus the agenda. Even the clients, who are paying an architect (one hopes) to produce drawings, rarely really understand what they are looking at.

Recognizing how important, and yet rare, drawing comprehension is, researchers at the Ecole Polytechnique Fédérale de Lausanne let residents of a housing community manipulate full-scale elements in a laboratory setting to help them better understand their new living spaces. One participant in the study, at the Laboratoire d'Expérimentation Architecturale (LEA), admitted "Someone in the trade of building can grasp things, but I do not see distances. I am not able to relate a size to a measure drawn on a plan."[20] Such experiments with one-to-one DIY modelling are increasingly taking place in augmented and virtual reality, with headsets and gloved hands manipulating elements in space. Both efforts suffer from a level of abstraction that keeps the experience of reality at bay: the Swiss study used large white plastic blocks with none of the smell, texture, or color of real materials, whereas AR and VR can give the image of color and texture, but no sense of physical presence (yet). Considering the time, labor, and capital invested in building, this lack of comprehension suggests that much of the client/architect relationship rests almost purely on faith. One might as well show potential concert ticket buyers the score for Beethoven's *Eroica* and ask, "So, how do you feel about the sound of this? Think it's worth the price?"

The very idea of a public and democratic process for the design and construction of other people's property is neither obvious nor universally accepted.[21] The world is full of buildings that were built despite or indifferent to the level of understanding of the parties involved. Yet we accept the world as we find it and grow accustomed to intrusions that we might have fought fiercely had their construction coincided with our lives. The construction of every building everywhere inconvenienced somebody at some point. The ubiquity and seemingly effortless existence of buildings eclipses the chaos and cacophony of the design and construction process: a chain link fence goes up around an empty lot or an abandoned building; earthmovers scrape away every trace of the past; and soon there's a sign posted with a rendering showing the new exciting building coming soon to your neighborhood (see Figure 1.5). Everyone's eyes turn to the rendering where thin, implausibly happy people stride purposefully through the suggestion of a sparkling and vibrant possible world, one that will *completely destroy* life as we know it. From that carefully crafted architectural image the anxious neighbor reads nothing but trucks, traffic, parking difficulties, new and different people—sometimes they're translucent—noise, litter, higher taxes, disrespect, and displacement. It doesn't "fit in." It means change. Architecture is Shiva, destroyer and maker of worlds.

Because architecture is a gregarious practice, much depends on how it is imagined and communicated, especially to the majority of people who are not

FIGURE 1.5 Note the helpful reminder that the "image is an artist's rendering," followed by a bit of legalese disclaiming.

themselves architects but who inhabit a world made by others on their behalf. The mystery is how *this*—a drawing or model—turns into *that*—a building, a landscape, a city. Architects and the public eye one another with mutual mistrust—the public worries that architects will screw up the places they love; architects worry that the public will beat their proposals into procrustean mediocrity. Despite what we architects might tell ourselves, architecture isn't for architects. It's for other people, most of whom are not equipped to understand from drawings what will be, or how it will be made, not to mention the agonies of construction. That standoff is no way to face a future of global urbanization, resource stress, climate change, and technological revolution. Besides, don't we all simply want beautiful buildings and cities?

As a design project draws closer to construction, the audience for the architect's graphic production expands. In the beginning only a small group—the client and the architect—needs to understand the drawings. Then the neighborhood NIMBYs, so aghast at the impending arrival of the thin happy people, are soon joined by the permit reviewers, code officials, zoning attorneys, mortgage lenders, construction managers, carpenters, plumbers, product suppliers, and the myriad trades required to build a building, and every one of them needs to discern his and her own role in the process and decipher their own pieces of the information. Even in this heterogeneous group of allied professions and trades, few read drawings and fewer still speak architecturese. Because it is the architect who is speaking in the drawings, it falls to her[22] to draft her language accordingly. And yet, that rarely happens.

For several years when I was beginning my academic career, I taught a summer course in a graduate program in real estate development. Pitched in the catalog as an "introduction to design," the course was required of any student who did not have a background in architecture. My challenge was to teach these folks—most of whom were already in the business of leasing, managing, commissioning, or trading buildings—a bit about how the things they were leasing, managing, commissioning, or trading came into this world. During a few of those summers at a different university, I was also teaching high school students who were entertaining thoughts of becoming architects. In my several summers with both groups, I discovered that future real estate executives are not so different from teenagers in many ways, not the least of which is being highly resistant to admitting ignorance. What set the two groups apart, though, was that the teenagers were interested in *becoming* architects; the real estate professionals, in *controlling* them.

Proficiencies in the language of drawing differed among my summer developers and teens, and the future architects I was teaching in fall and spring, in the same way the ability to read music differs among the professional musician, the promoter, and the devoted fan. This became clear when I walked the developers through a set of drawings and asked them if they knew how to navigate from building plans and sections to details to understand the building's construction. This was an important step for the class; construction drawings, unlike promotional renderings, are legal documents so the comprehension of what is being said in drawing and writing has real consequence. Yet, many of my students didn't understand how to use the alphanumeric combinations in little circles and arrows to work their way from drawing to drawing. The graphic language of architectural drawing was like a foreign language to them. They knew just enough to be dangerous, like knowing how to order a beer, but not how to ask where the toilet is.

Architecture is a language. In fact, we in the architecture community hear that so many times we might think that we understand what that statement means. Is it actually a language, with elements and rules governing their combinations in such a way that architecture can bear meaning? Or is it a "language" metaphorically? We assume that cloaked behind that simple declaration is sufficient understanding of both architecture and language that each basks in the reflected illumination of the other. From historians such as John Summerson through various deconstructionists, architectural theorists have focused on the grammar of the building itself, focusing either on its semantics in order to demonstrate the presence or absence of legible meaning inhering in architectural elements, or its syntax, to revel in the rules and relations among architectural elements independent of meaning.[23] Despite the wishes of the post-modernist classicists, it turns out that the purported timeless meanings of columns, arches, and pediments are subject to the same semantic drift as the meanings in any other language. Architecture communicates in many ways, sometimes like an elephant, in subsonic frequencies that we can't hear but only feel, and rarely exactly as intended. Architecture may be a language, but its elements are conceived in another medium, drawing, which is different in almost every way from the medium of building itself.

Architecture is a language, and architectural drawing is a language, but they are not exactly the same, nor are either "natural" languages. That is the term for the languages we acquire naturally, through use and exposure, growing up, and being in the world. We use our natural languages unreflectively for the most part, their naturalness blinding us to their underlying complexities. Only when we try to learn another language do we realize how difficult it is. (If English weren't my natural language, I wonder if I would be able to learn it; it's a mess.) The fact that we use that adjective "natural" to modify a particular form of language underlines the fact that there are *unnatural* languages. Notation systems for music, dance, and even the Xs and Os of football are unnatural languages, the goals of which are to establish some kind of meaningful relation to the world. So it is with architectural drawings.

What exactly is architectural drawing, if it is something entirely different from other kinds of drawing? What does it communicate? To whom and how? To talk about drawing and language monolithically as we have been doing is a bit misleading, for there are several languages and types of drawing, nested and related to one another in complex ways. Moreover, drawings, words, and even numbers, entangle themselves tightly in certain types of architectural drawing. There is a language of drawing, a language of architecture, and this—the words you are reading now—the natural language of talking about both, individually and jointly. They relate to one another in what William Mitchell called a triangular pattern of reference, in which our sentences and words describe things in the design world, and things in the design world stand in, instantiate, for things in the constructed world.[24] Mitchell suggests—although I'm not sure I agree with him on this—that our sentences rest first on the design world and refer only "indirectly to the real world."[25] In other words, there are things and there is talk about things. Furthermore, within the category "things," there are things that stand for the other things. The words and the things-that-stand-for-things are representations of the things of the (real) construction world (see Figure 1.6). They are all related, but they should

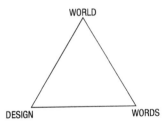

FIGURE 1.6   The triangular pattern of reference, based on William Mitchell's diagram.

not be confused for one another. No one could mistake the word "column" for a real one or a drawn one.

Even so, in design studio, client meetings, or public presentations, architects tend to talk directly to the content of the image as if the lines, tones, and marks were neutral and transparent, and they were talking about the architecture itself. An architect points at a *drawing* of a stair, but in her mind and in her language she's pointing at a *stair*, as if the real thing has materialized (see Figure 1.7). She

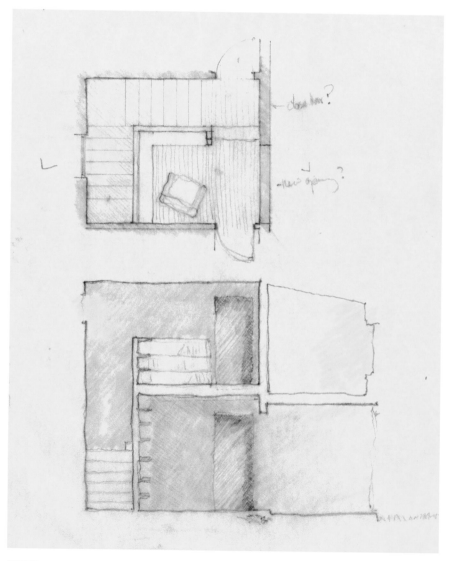

FIGURE 1.7   Or the stair could be like this…

may say, while pointing, something like, "visitors go up here to the library," using a mode of language that appears to be describing an actual stair in a factual situation. Moreover, her drawings are speaking on their own, *sotto voce*, with varying degrees of certainty depending on their technique and media. If the drawing of the stair is a pencil sketch drawn freehand and full of little inconsistencies, the drawing whispers, "it could be sorta like this, or not…I don't know." If the stair is drafted and dimensioned, it insists, "this is the way it's going to be; you're going to go up here, turn and go up again." In a later chapter, we'll talk about the full expressive range of those whispers—sometimes there's shouting—and how media and technique can really change the conversation.

Usually we look *through* the drawing to the drawn, and try to ignore the whispering. Social scientist and philosopher Donald Schön describes this phenomenon, the ability to "use graphic languages transparently," as a learned procedure: the architect "sees through [it]…just as practiced readers can see through the letters on a page to words and meanings."[26] Like language or speech—those two are different—though, these drawings are not neutral. They are pre-loaded with intentionality, whether or not the architect realizes it. You're reading these words right now: does the choice of font, the color of the ink, or their arrangement on the page carry any hidden messages to you, or are you looking straight through the writing to the written?

It is here, in the land of linguistics, where we consider the relationship between representations and their objects, between sign and signifier, between the thing and the talk about the thing. That is what's most interesting about Mitchell's triumvirate of representation; it's not only the points of the triangle, it's also the unnamed legs that connect them, the "about" in "talk about" and the "of" in "drawings of." The prepositions are at least as interesting as the nouns. For example, the word "column" exists in what Mitchell calls the critical language, but which we could also just call natural language, and names one of the fundamental elements of architecture. Within the design and construction community, a shared understanding exists of what that natural language word signifies in both the world of design media and the world as constructed. Say the word "column" to any architect, builder, or engineer and there will be nods of understanding. Yet, our comfort with the word "column" and our shared understanding of what we mean when we say it masks one of the persistent epistemological problems of language, that of concepts and percepts.[27] In other words, the word "column" in this context describes a concept, a class of things that share a set of characteristics that distinguish them from anything else. People in the design professions know enough about those characteristics not to mix up "column" with "beam," but we can't assume that everyone does. A non-professional might confuse them because they are both linear things that hold buildings up. A percept column is, in contrast to a concept column, a particular column one may know, like Foster's extremely thin columns in Nîmes (see Figure 1.8). There is a definition of

FIGURE 1.8   Classical columns and their thin descendants at the 1993 Carré d'Art by Foster+ Partners, Nîmes, France. Photo by Douglas R. Palladino

"column"—an element that bears compressive forces collinearly along its vertical axis—but its definition does not *prescribe* its manifestation in drawing or building. Instead, its definition *proscribes* an almost infinite set of things that don't fit the basic definition and leaves available a spectrum of possible columns that meet the definition and also do many more things *because* they meet the definition.

The concept of column brings with it various architectural qualities and properties that are the results, or side effects even, of the nature of the column. Between any two columns exists the space known as the intercolumniation. To the ancients, this figural absence was part of the column; its measure was tied to the order that bore it. In conventional modern construction, it is a nameless nothingness, determined more often than not by the statics and strengths of the material used in the horizontal span, or by the percentage of the budget available for structure. In either case, the space comes with the column, no extra charge, so the concept of column includes qualities of permeability and openness. The magnification or minimization of those qualities occurs at the level of the percept of column, but they are already present in the concept. Other qualities follow from the definition of the concept and are equally as absent as the space between: the beams that are needed to make of the column something more than a totem, the lateral stabilization that any system constructed of points and lines needs to stand, etc.

The difference between concept and percept becomes clear when we translate the word to drawing. Ask a group of architects—or architecture students, as I have done—to draw what they see in their mind's eyes when they hear the word "column" (see Figures 1.9, 1.10, and 1.11). As soon as pencil hits paper,

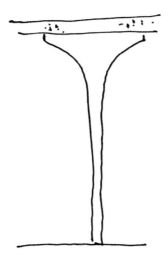

FIGURE 1.9   A student drawing's percept of a column, in answer to the prompt, "draw a column."

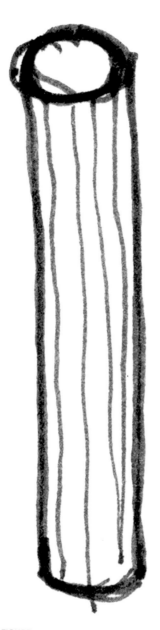

FIGURE 1.10   Another student's percept of a column.

ideological biases, personal taste, knowledge of history, travel, experience, etc. will sweep away the concept of column and leave a drawing of a percept, a specific thing that may or may not look anything like what we have in *our* mind when we say the word. You can't actually draw a concept; you can only draw a percept.

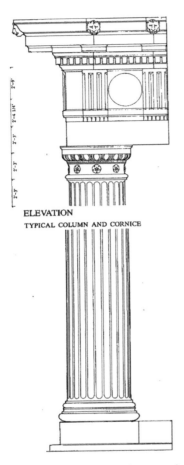

ELEVATION
TYPICAL COLUMN AND CORNICE

FIGURE 1.11   Someone else's percept of a column.

This may sound like the kind of obscure rumination that academics enjoy, with little bearing on real practice or just an architect's party game—go ahead, try it on your friends!—but consider what might happen in a conversation among architect, client and contractor about an unseen and undrawn column, perhaps to be deployed in a colonnade for the front of a building. Each may nod in knowing agreement that a colonnade would look wonderful, but the mind's image of each column in the colonnade may be so radically different that the real trouble will begin inevitably when the architect draws his percept colonnade and the client sees how different it is from hers. It matters which bison is which.

In this book, we're going to try to steer clear of talking about architecture itself, least of all whether any given work is "good" or not. Yet, *how* we draw does have a profound influence on the buildings we make, so we will be interrogating the stuff that architects make on the way to architecture—drawings of all shapes, sizes, and flavors, models both physical and digital, and even words and number in their problematic relationship to drawings. These works have audiences, and those audiences differ over time. At first an architect and her drawings are in close conversation only with each other, speaking in the kind of shorthand reserved for intimates. As the design develops, the boss, the intern, and the colleague require a bit more expository drawing, but they all speak the same language like a family with its own insider slang. Architecture, however, depends for its existence on a client, and communicating with him requires a conscious shift, a modification—if not an outright translation—of the graphic and spoken languages. This is not to disparage the client. There is no reason for someone who is not in the design world to be fluent in the design language. Architects should understand that by now; our impenetrable jargon has become a pop culture cliché (see Figure 1.12). Each of the issues raised here will appear again, in depth, in the following chapters.

Any discussion of drawing, communications, or image-making in general immediately gets one entangled in a conversation that has been going on for thousands of years, a conversation that may even precede natural language, which makes it very hard for our logocentric minds to imagine. Like an inhabitant of Italo Calvino's city of Ersilia[28], every idea in this book is connected to the ideas and theories of others, some with heavy rope, others with the frailest filaments. To make any progress at all we will have to cut some of those strings and let the loose ends fall, knowing that when we do, we will, as Jacob Bronowski says, "do violence to connections in the world."[29] Readers who want to take their own regress to the truth and beauty discussions of Plato and Aristotle may put the book down at any time and do so on their own.

Why should we care how drawings work? And who is *we*? Architects and designers should care because drawings are our language and they have a greater and more nuanced expressive range than we give them credit for. Citizens of the built environment should care too, because we inhabit a world in which images of all kinds—photographs, manipulated or not, infographics, simulations, and animations—fill our view and increasingly dominate words. Images carry messages in complex ways, silently yet persistently persuading us, and shaping our perspective of the current and future world. We can just wallow in the delight of them, the way we might enjoy listening to a conversation in Italian without any concern for real comprehension, but wouldn't we prefer to understand, to be graphically literate, if not fluent?

By drawing, we make in order to make; in other words, it is our intention by making a drawing to induce the making of something else. Drawings can and do make the world. We draw for all the same reasons that we write and talk—to remember, to imagine, to describe, to imitate, to elaborate, to beseech, to promise, to wish, to instruct, and to change the world. Theories of natural language and communication, then, offer productive analogies to figure out exactly

FIGURE 1.12   Would that this were true. Speed Bump cartoon ©Dave Coverly

how drawings work, how they do all these things…how drawings can change the world. In the following chapters we will exercise that analogy to illuminate different types of drawings (noun) and different modes of drawing (verb), and you will enjoy a refresher course in grammar along the way.

NOTES

1. In English, the words "cave bison" mean a particular type of bison; in Latin "cave bison" would mean "beware of bison." Hmm. More than coincidence?

2. All of this bison material comes from an article "Early cave art and ancient DNA record the origin of European bison," published in *Nature Communications* in 2016.

3. "The diversity of bison representations has been explained as putative cultural and individual variation of style through time, since the steppe bison was assumed to be the only bison present in Late Paleolithic Europe." Ibid, P 2.

4. Ibid.

5. Ibid, P 6.

6. Ibid, P 2. Geneticists have tried to verify the existence of other prehistoric subjects beyond the bison. A paper in *Proceedings of the National Academy of Sciences* titled "Genotypes of predomestic horses match phenotypes painted in Paleolithic works of cave art" notes "Thus, all horse color phenotypes that seem to be distinguishable in cave paintings have now been found to exist in prehistoric horse populations, suggesting that cave paintings of this species represent remarkably realistic depictions of the animals shown. This finding lends support to hypotheses arguing that cave paintings might have contained less of a symbolic or transcendental connotation than often assumed."

7. Kandinsky had laid out the argument for what came to be known as non-objective art in 1910 in his book *On the Spiritual in Art*, and it all just took off from there...do I really need to get into that here? Consult any art history text.

8. Pliny, XXXV, P 15: *Aegyptii sex milibus annorum aput ipsos inventam...*

9. Ibid.

10. Ibid, P 150. He also credits Butades's father with inventing relief sculpture, by using clay to make his daughter's outline more lifelike. Beyond the origin myth, there are two things truly captivating about this story: one, how touching is the loving gesture by her father; two, that drawing was invented by a woman. Wow. Why does no one talk about that part?

11. Goodman, *Languages of Art*, P 36.

12. I've been talking about drawings and paintings as if there were no difference between the two. For our purposes here, there really isn't. A painting is a two-dimensional image made of paint; a drawing is a two dimensional image made of...draw? These are differences of technique, rather than world-relating, in translating an image to a flat surface.

13. The scientist Felisa Wolfe-Simon is quoted in "Scientist in a Strange Land" by Tom Clynes in *Popular Science*.

14. www.scientificamerican.com/article.cfm?id=how-artists-portray-exoplanets-never-seen. In an email correspondence with me, artist Lynette Cook warned that digital technologies have only further blurred "the line between reality and science-based conjecture."

15. Ibid.

16. Ibid.

17. Goodman, *Languages of Art*, P 34.

18. It is surprisingly difficult to listen and look at something at the same time. The two kinds of information tend to interfere with each other, in a variation of the so-called Perky Effect. Google it. It's fascinating.

19. For one of the few in-depth studies of the design review process see Brenda Scheer's & Wolfgang Preiser's anthology *Design Review: Challenging Urban Aesthetic Control*.

20. Lawrence, "Laypeople as Architectural Designers," P 236.

21. See Scheer's *Design Review* again for a variety of legal challenges to the public process.

22. I'm alternating pronouns to avoid any consistent gender assignments. Sometime she's the architect and he's the client; other times, the other way round. Draw no conclusions. Gender is in fact an issue in language and communication, but that's a bit outside my current subject.
23. Summerson, Eisenman, Mitchell, Benedikt... The list is long.
24. Mitchell, *The Logic of Architecture*, P 64.
25. Ibid. Mitchell quickly replaces the phrase "real world" with "construction world" so as not to become mired in arcane ontological problems. On that I couldn't agree more.
26. Schön, *The Reflective Practitioner*, P 159.
27. See C. S. Peirce, *The Essential Writings* for a thorough survey of the problem.
28. Calvino, *Invisible Cities*, P 76.
29. Bronowski, *The Origins of Knowledge and Imagination*, P 58–59.

CHAPTER 2
RHETORIC AND PERSUASION

The human imagination is an amazing instrument; it allows our minds to wander in space and time, contemplating bison and exoplanets, even as our bodies are completely still. I can imagine myself in London at Covent Garden in summer while I sit hunched at this computer in Alexandria in winter (see Figure 2.1). My imagining is supported by my memory of having in fact been at Covent Garden in summer. Imagining now that I am back there, I'm not remembering any particular moment or event, so much as just being there, remembering the sounds of street musicians and hawkers, the smells from restaurants, the look and feel of the cobbled pavement. Teasing apart which bits are memories and which bits are imagined, though, is impossible. It's always sunny in my mind, and I know that can't possibly be an accurate memory of London. What differentiates a visualized memory from an imagined vision? In my remembered Covent Garden I can't zoom into a mental image and peer around corners or open doors that I didn't open when I was there. Thanks to Google, I have an image in my mind that includes Covent Garden from the air, even though I myself have never hovered above it. I can't query my visual memory for details that I didn't see at the time, but I can, however, imagine myself opening a door, walking up a stair, and into the sky above, and then I'm inventing, rather than remembering. I'm imagining a new geography. My Covent Garden is a mosaic of my experiences there, my recollections of having looked at my own photographs, as well as other images I've seen produced by others. It's a mix of memory and imagination.

In his beautiful little book *Thinking Architecture*, Peter Zumthor writes about how memory and imagination entangle in his design process:

> When I design a building, I frequently find myself sinking into old, half-forgotten memories... And although I cannot trace any special forms, there is a hint of fullness and of richness which makes me think: this I have seen before. Yet, at the same time, I know that it is all new and different, and that there is no direct reference to a former work of architecture which might divulge the secret of the memory-laden mood.[1]

FIGURE 2.1   I remember being there, in Covent Garden…Photo by Douglas R. Palladino

This I have seen before. Yes, but not exactly. We all have heads stuffed full of memories constructed from singular experiences of real places, pressed through the sieve of personal expectations. Some of us—writers and architects, for example—hoard these memories because we know they will all come in handy in the future. Everything is material. Architects travel, sometimes to monument-chase, sometimes to seek out, like Captain Kirk and his crew, strange new worlds. With camera, sketchbook, eyes and body, the architect feeds on the built world and, in so doing, makes it her own.

There is a Villa Savoy out there in suburban Paris, swaddled in its own iconicity, but every architect who has seen it has constructed her own remembered Villa Savoy, flavored by the surprise of seeing it in its actual context, rather than tightly cropped in the Corbusian literature. How does that experience, the personal and professional knowledge of the Villa Savoy, leak into that architect's next project for a house in suburban Washington? Does it matter if the memories show? If the references are too literal, the work is derivative; too oblique, and they are invisible? Is it helpful for the architect to mention her Corbusian inspiration when she shows her clients the sketches for their new house? Does that reference act like a prestige contagion, infecting the drawings to make them more authoritative, and therefore more persuasive? Architecture is not expository writing, however, and neither footnotes nor extensive bibliographies confer authority nor ensure quality. Moreover, buildings once built do not come with indexed back matter through which an inhabitant or visitor can flip to check on the correctness of their own interpretations.

Citizens of architecture, a category that includes but is not limited to clients, put their heads stuffed full of memories to very different uses than do architects, more for reference and comparison than as source material. If Zumthor gives voice to the architect's alchemy of memory and imagination, philosopher and writer Gaston Bachelard speaks for the others, the clients, both intentional and inadvertent: "...there exists for each one of us an oneiric house, a house of dream-memory, that is lost in the shadow of a beyond of the real past."[2] The definition of that word—oneiric—is something pertaining to dreams, but Bachelard makes his own compound word of dream-memory, which keeps the oneiric in this usage tethered to experience. While Bachelard focuses on the psycho-geography of the childhood house, there are, I would argue, outer rings of the oneiric. There also exists for each of us an oneiric street, neighborhood, town, and city, cobbled together from those early dream-memories of the world outside of the home. The sense of being "at home" is not limited to being physically in a home. Bachelard reminds us that "the house we were born in is physically inscribed in us."[3] Using drawing as metaphor—"inscribed" means to be drawn or written into—he continues: the house is not only "inscribed," but the house has "engraved within us the hierarchy of the various functions of inhabiting, and all the other houses are but variations on a fundamental theme."[4] Thus, every act of creative reinvention—or to be a Marxist about it, creative destruction—whether of the house-type, the structure of the street, the definition of neighborhood, or the assembly of cities, chips away at the wholeness of our oneiric.

Born in the tiny and cinematically charming French town of Bar-sur-Aube in 1888, Bachelard lived until 1962, a span of architectural time during which ideology, economy, and technology systematically flattened and rationalized his garrets, attics, and cellars—if they hadn't already been flattened by world war. A contemporary reader, particularly an American one, might relegate to history all these attics and garrets and cellars through which French boys at the *fin de siècle* prowled while daydreaming. Modernism freed us from the burden of history and, in so doing, basted the oneiric in nostalgia. The post-war house-scape of the United States is considerably different from the world of Bachelard's childhood in France. Not all oneiric places are as appealing as his. Some of us grew up without attics or cellars—forget about garrets—in slab-on-grade ranch houses that populated monocultural subdivisions circumscribed by arterial roads. We spent our leisure time at faux-colonial shopping malls not the tranquil banks of the river Aube. Our contemporary flattened, rational world is where many Americans feel "at home" and thus, if the marketers are to be believed, that's what they want. Now that's serious oneiric baggage.

We carry this phenomenological luggage with us everywhere we go and we go a lot of places and we go often. We would like to think that our choices of where to live, in what neighborhood, and in what type of dwelling, are rational; that we weigh various combinations of fixed and variable costs, proximities, and amenities. Yet the constant drone of the oneiric exerts its profound pull. The "home-building"[5] industry plays to our dream-memories with shrewd word-image combinations that ping our emotions like sonar, deploying a set of architectural style widgets in freestyle combinations: various layers of pitched roofs that promise Bachelardian attics, a smattering of shutters, porch-ish appendages, and of course, arched windows, those persistent signifiers of class. These images are usually photographs of built model-houses, something that only the industrialized house production machine can afford to do. In this way, an architect who could design a unique house for a client—for the sake of argument, let's say for the same price, which is certainly possible—is at a disadvantage immediately. She must persuade with drawings, while the "home-builder" can persuade with a visit to a real example, or at least a photograph of same. In a persuasion face-off between drawings and photographs, the latter has always had the advantage.[6]

I have been simplistically dividing the population into two camps, architects and non-architects, which at first might seem about as helpful as dividing the population into people who play the guitar and people who don't, but it's more interesting than that. At some point, certain people unpack their oneiric baggage and decide to do something with—or about, or to—the physical world. Whether to shake off the chains of their memory places or shape the world to more closely align with them, some people become architects.[7] That changes forever their—our—relation to the world. Bachelard, a polymath who was seemingly everything but an architect, sounds a lot like one when he says "Space calls for action, and before action, the imagination is at work."[8] It is the call for action that separates the architect from the others. Everyone can imagine; everyone can remember; but not everyone, having imagined and remembered, acts.

Space calls for action, but not just any kind of action. Even though architects have been often mythologized as solitary geniuses—a truly counterproductive myth—making architecture is not a solitary activity. It is gregarious or, to use Nelson Goodman's terminology, allographic[9]. Unlike such lonely pursuits as writing poetry or painting, which Goodman calls autographic activities, architecture's execution depends entirely on the labors of others.[10] The architect's primary task, then, is to get other people to do things. The action—the things that need doing—encompasses far more than simply getting the construction crew to pay attention to the drawings, although that is critical. Before action, the imagination is at work. What will this building look like? How will it rest on the earth? What will the rooms feel like? Where is the sun? Will I hear my neighbors or smell their cooking? Will it fit in or stand out? Before construction can even begin, then, many others beyond just the architect and his client must be able to share in the imagining—colleagues, consultants, clients, neighbors, financiers, insurers, bankers, permit reviewers, cost estimators, and design review boards. Everyone involved in this collective pre-construction vision comes to the proverbial table with their own unique sets of oneiric luggage, the contents of which are unpacked and laid out next to the new imaginings in order to measure the alignments to, and variations from, each one's dream-memory. "It is," as Zumthor says, "all new and different" but through drawings, models, and words, the architect must persuade each person along the way to join him in imagining this new world. To talk about this—how to get a group of people with diverse points of view and agendas to support something that they can't yet see in its entirety—we have to invoke a whole category of functional linguistics to look at conditionals, performatives, agency, authority, the nature of directives, and of course, the arts of persuasion in general, usually referred to as rhetoric.

First, a confession: I had really hoped to avoid taking the long hike back to Aristotle, yet as soon as I uttered the word "rhetoric" I knew I'd have to read *Rhetoric*. Granted, Aristotle has a lot to say about the world and our relation to it, but do we always have to cite a source that's over twenty five hundred years old? If I start bringing Aristotle into my arguments, then I have to come clean on the fact that I only know his writing through a little Penguin Classics paperback I picked up at a discount from the now-defunct Books-A-Million, and that any quote I might include exists at the tail end of a much stretched coily-cord in a scholarly game of telephone—and that's a metaphor that is itself obsolete. I don't read Greek, classical or otherwise, yet here I am, beginning this chapter on rhetoric and persuasion, which leads me straight back to Aristotle.

Most architects would rather not be herded into the same corral as politicians, but if we are talking about persuasion and rhetoric, that is where they belong. Architects' particular form of rhetoric is political, because, as Aristotle says, "political speaking urges us either to do or not to do something" and that political rhetoric—as opposed to the other two flavors of rhetoric, forensic and ceremonial oratory—"is concerned with the future."[11] Architecture as a practice and as a made thing in the world, is fundamentally political; no matter the size of the building, it controls, organizes, and represents capital, resources, and human labor. And architecture is fundamentally concerned with the future; even if it happens to be a project focused on the preservation of an older building, it is focused on the future of that past. It's no surprise, then, that the architect's persuasive efforts should fall under the political rhetoric. But the architect's rhetoric differs significantly from the politician's in the media of its delivery and the problematic relationships among those media. In short, the architect will use words, diagrams, drawings, physical models, digital representations, film—just about anything he can get his hands on and his ideas into—to enroll an audience in his propositions. The dangerous part lies in the tightrope of credibility on which the images walk.

The purpose of all this persuading, according to Aristotle, is happiness:

> It may be said that every individual man and all men in common aim at a certain end which determines what they choose and what they avoid. This end, to sum it up briefly, is happiness and its constituents… For all advice to do things or not to do them is concerned with happiness and with the things that make for or against it; whatever creates or increases happiness or some part of happiness, we ought to do; whatever destroys or hampers happiness, or gives rise to its opposite, we ought not to do.[12]

Alas, if only it were so simple. Our goal here isn't to determine what makes people happy, nor am I interested in even trying to define "happiness." Rather, we need to take a close look at how architects can persuade people that they will be happy, or at least *happier*—however they define that state of being—if they approve, pay for, support, or at least stop obstructing and lawyering-up to fight, a given project.

Why do certain projects sail unscathed through the straits of public and regulatory approval while others founder or emerge changed and beaten, missing a few floors and burdened with some ameliorating stylistic flourishes? It isn't always because of inherent objective merit or architectural quality. The sheer number of mediocre buildings in the world stands as mute evidence that it isn't always the best that gets built. Instead, certain architects are simply much better than others are at marshaling and coordinating the full complement of rhetorical tools—graphic, verbal, and personal—necessary to make a persuasive case.

Rhetorical. We really have to redeem that word. To call something rhetorical today is to dismiss it as applied excess, redundant, words for words' sake. Rhetoric has become a synonym for verbal ornamentation, for spin, bulls**t, and therefore an object of suspicion. We think we're being sold, snowed, offered up a tangle of inspiration and persuasion successfully obscuring any content.[13] This is an unfortunate degradation of the classical definition of rhetoric as the art(s) of persuasion; it is substantive language, directed toward action, toward motivating others to act, to be moved. True rhetoric, whether in verbal or graphic form, is built on an accurate reading of the situation and a reflective understanding of possibilities. In this way, a drawing is political rather than fanciful.

The language of architecture before construction, when it is in the design stages, sits somewhere between poetry and rhetoric, at least as Aristotle has defined them. There seem to be some fuzzy boundaries between the two. Political rhetoric is directed toward the future rather than describing things that have happened, which is the job of the forensic orator. Meanwhile, in *Poetics* Aristotle distinguishes between the historian and the poet, saying that "the function of the poet is not to say what *has* happened, but to say the kind of thing that *would* happen."[14] And here is where things get interesting. These two proclamations about the purposes of political rhetoric and poetry start to feel very similar as both turn their respective gazes away from the past and toward a desired/desirable future. Only rhetoric, however, calls for action: to do or do not, as Yoda would put it. Poetry, for all its virtues, does not.

To crawl back from ancient Greece to our own possible futures, we might have to leave the Aristotelian distinctions between poetry and rhetoric behind and begin to think of design as fiction: a story of a particular place and particular people, and how their lives change under the new circumstances illustrated here by the architect. The function of the drawings and other design media then, to put it more colloquially, is get people to buy into the story. To be effective at persuasion, at getting the buy-in, architects have to become more nimble with languages.

In his book *Why Architects Draw*, Ed Robbins talks about drawings as rhetoric:

> Not only the dominant instrument of social and technical discourse within architectural production, drawing is also the primary rhetorical medium of the discourse. If rhetoric is the art of persuasive discourse, then the drawing is the form architects use to frame their rhetorical strategies.[15]

Shortly thereafter, however, he slips from the classical definition of rhetoric, the art of persuasion, leaving the "persuasion" part behind and heads straight into the "art" part, positing a "whole new set of possible social roles for architects as critics, as visionaries, and as artistic fantasists."[16] Citing the drawings of Lebbeus Woods, Robbins says that such drawings are meant as "only rhetorical and not an actual architectural production."[17] That dismissive qualifier "only" sends us back to where the rhetorical suggests "unreal" or "fanciful" and strips away the call to action. Aristotle reminds us that even in poetry, which has a far more generous spectrum of allowable fantasy, "probable impossibilities are preferable to

31

implausible possibilities," and that "stories should not be constructed from irrational parts."[18] What does that mean, that a drawing should not be constructed from "irrational parts"? And what is the thin pencil line between "probable impossibilities" and "implausible possibilities"? Like words in a sentence, the architect's lines and marks have to respect a grammar, a set of rules for how certain things have to be represented. Furthermore, the representations have to have sufficient correspondence to the real world that one can evaluate their relative probability and plausibility. And, those rules and conventions for representations and correspondences have to be learned; they are not part of natural language.

I always carry a simple number-two pencil around in my hand while I'm at school, walking from desk crit to desk crit[19]. I realized early in my teaching career that, oddly, you couldn't count on students having pencils readily available at their desks—even more so now in the so-called digital studio—and, in any case, after using a few that looked well chewed, it seemed best to bring my own.[20] At the typical desk crit, the student does a lot of talking while shuffling paper or poking at the computer screen. I, in turn, do a lot of listening, talking, and asking them to poke at a different part of their screen. Sometimes, words aren't sufficient and I need that number-two pencil just to draw something. I code-switch.

Code-switching is the sociolinguistic term to describe how bi-/multi-lingual people can switch effortlessly between languages, using first one then the other, sometimes in one sentence. There are many theories of why people do this, from the extremely pragmatic—there's just no English word that can replace *schadenfreuede*—to the socio-cultural, in order to establish either allegiance with or distance from others. Architects are constantly code-switching between their two languages—speaking and drawing—with varying degrees of mastery and effectiveness. Becoming architecturally bilingual is the first challenge for architecture students. Accepting these two languages *qua* languages, Donald Schön describes design as a "reflective conversation with the situation," a conversation that is carried out in both languages. In his chapter on architecture, which is in fact titled "Design as a Reflective Conversation with the Situation," Schön himself code-switches, by including diagrammatic line drawings interspersed with the text.[21]

The desk crit is the object of his study, so Schön observes the interactions between an architecture student and her professor, and describes their communication: "His [the professor's] words do not describe what is already there on the paper but parallel the processes by which he makes what is there."[22] The lines of the drawings, he goes on, "are unclear in their reference except insofar as he says what they mean. His words are obscure except insofar as Petra [the student] can connect them with the lines of the drawing."[23] And, Schön's words are likewise unclear without the drawings. He admits to the reader that, "we must reconstruct Quist's [the professor] pointing and drawing, referring to the sketches which accompany the transcript and, on occasion, making new sketches which clarify Quist's meanings."[24] Schön is both transcriber and translator here, faithfully reproducing the words and sketches of the protocol, but then having to translate Quist's "dychtic utterances—'here,' 'this,' 'that,'—which Petra can interpret only by observing his movements."[25]

Everything in this reflective conversation is an utterance—the words, the marks, the gestures, the translated diagrams—and each is loaded with meaning. Each utterance is irreducible, as Quist and Petra narrow the field of their conversation so that they are referring to this world and only this world, the design problem at hand. Linguists would call these irreducible utterances *morphemes*, meaning-units more elemental even than words. This, that, here—these are morphemes and physical marks on paper. You're looking at them right now, reading. Yet we think of their making as quite different; I'm typing these words on a screen—there isn't really any "paper"—so the marks are made instantly, flawlessly, each "m" the same as every other "m." But sketches don't look like that at all (see Figure 2.2), and even with words, this was not always the case. Illuminated manuscripts, calligraphy, the old concept of penmanship, these all associated the craft of making marks with the content of the utterance. We marvel at someone's ability to sketch from life, but don't give a second thought to how she forms letters in a journal.[26]

For drawings, then, it may be more useful to talk about *graphemes*, the marks on paper that carry and construct meanings. In an architectural drawing, the question is: how few of these marks and lines, and in what combinations, does one need to make meaning? How few lines does an architect need to distill a set

FIGURE 2.2   Every sketch of this building would be slightly different, even if one were traced from another. That would not be the case for a digital drawing.

of spatial, structural, and functional variables? Let's begin with three graphemes, a fat line, a thin line, and a dot (see Figure 2.3). When described that way, as lines and dots, and arrayed on a page thus, these marks are unmoored to any architectural meaning. They lie on the page, linked only by propinquity, just a fat line, a thin line, and a dot. But, arrange them as in Figure 2.4 and they begin to speak. Transmogrified from just a mark with a geometrical definition—the shortest distance between two points—the line is now loaded with propositional content and can no longer be called a line.[27] The fat line has become a wall-like element, made of solid stuff, continuous and unbroken, suggesting it could bear weight. The thin line shares some propositional content with its fat friend: it is also continuous and suggests a suite of possible slim materials, but it doesn't look capable of bearing any weight. Looking no more substantial than the edge of a piece of paper, it can only contour, wrap and enclose. The thin line—can we read it as glass or a screen?—needs the dots, which we now draft into service as columns, to be of any architectural use. If we then add the magic ingredient of dashed lines[28]—our fourth grapheme—we can see beams (see Figure 2.5). This is how a fat line, a thin line, and a few dots together cohere into a grapheme—an architectural morpheme—a unit of architectural meaning.

These deceptively simple little sketches are meaning-multipliers; each arrangement lays out a likely sequence of possibilities and relationships, while warning of the foreclosure of others. Meaning even leaks out onto the surrounding paper; the neutral nothingness of the paper's surface is now differentiated between what is inside the walls—the marks are no longer lines—and what is outside.

FIGURE 2.3   A fat line, a thin line, and a dot.

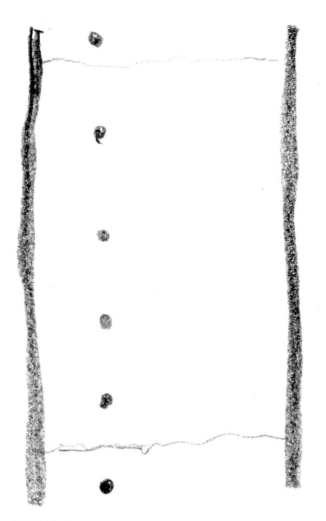

FIGURE 2.4   Two walls, enclosure, and a line of columns.

Paper space has become latent place, or *site*. Our initial set of three graphemes, baby's first utterances, now together say "rowhouse," a spatio-structural-cultural category of building that links the private world lived between walls to the exquisite complexities of city-making. There is the implication of how they can or can't be assembled into more complex sentences. An architect with a head stuffed full of memories looks at that fat line, thin line, and row of dots and sees the inexhaustible theme and variations from the masonry street walls of Back Bay to the unctuous "townhomes" of Outer Asphaltia, and through that to the technological, social, and cultural evolutions to which the rowhouse is subject.

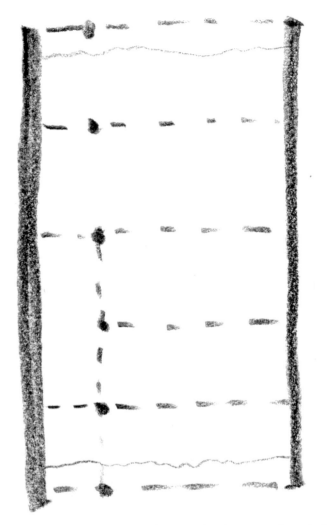

FIGURE 2.5   The dashed lines bring beams into the conversation and with them come implications of three-dimensional space.

I am calling my sketch a meaningful arrangement of graphemes, but most architects would call it a "*parti*," an enigmatic word we toss around as if all listeners are equally knowledgeable about its meaning and, as with the language of classical ballet, appreciate it all the more because it must remain in French. It's clear that even architecture students aren't entirely sure what the word means. They often confuse it with "party," not as in what they do after studio, but as in "party walls," the shared solid boundaries (remember the fat line) that separate the private spaces in rowhouses and also join the houses together into a larger whole. Students often refer to these instead as *"parti* walls." While both words have architectural currency, and descend from the same Latin root word *partire,* which means to separate, they don't buy the same meaning. Yet the confusion has some inadvertent value; the rowhouse *parti* depends on the representation of party walls. That's what makes it a rowhouse, and that's the clue to what a *parti* is: a spatio-tectonic diagram.

Design often begins in diagrams because at the start of a project only so much is given to the architect: a site, meaning someplace on earth where the project is supposed to go; a list of stuff the client wants the building to do; maybe a list of stuff the neighbors don't want it to do; and a budget that satisfies no one. All diagrams are not equal, however; some suggest form, others relationships, and others still are what architects like to call "conceptual," meaning a diagram that should not be read as representing the actual building so much as ideas about it. According to architectural mythology, these often appear on cocktail napkins. A *parti* sketch is silent on function, in the same way that a so-called "bubble diagram," (see Figure 2.6) is silent on form. Bubble diagrams, which are not as charming and festive as they sound, are "systems of lines and circles used in architecture to show relationships between functional areas of a program to develop an archi-tectural plan."[29] A bubble diagram is a first draft translation of words and numbers into graphic form, bounding words like "entry," "living room," "deck" with lines and then arranging them, like concrete poetry, into a rough approximation of how they might want to be. Their bubbly quality is intentional, to resist the suggestion of architectural form. Their content is solely directed toward relationships such as proximity, grouping, and clustering; in that sense, bubble diagrams are topological, with no quantitative measure. The substantive difference between the *parti* and the bubble condenses the problematic relationship between form and function.

Form and function, architecture's chicken and egg, have never managed to settle into an accepted causal relationship, but the requirement that the former obediently follow the latter is one of the dominant rhetorical tropes of Modernism. The familiar phrase "form follows function" comes from Louis Sullivan, but the alliterative conjunction of the two words predates him by a half century, appearing in the title of a book by sculptor Horatio Greenough.[30] Greenough expended many well-chosen words dismissing the art and architecture of his peers for, among other things, being pathetically derivative of European models. His language—and his point—will be familiar to anyone who has read Sullivan or Frank Lloyd Wright, or who has drunk the functionalist Kool-Aid. He argues that there are reasons for the way things look in nature, the way animals and plants are formed, and that adherence to nature's model is the only way forward for an authentic architecture. He also argues, as innumerable critics and historians have done previously for their own purposes, that architecture's "decline"—it's always a present problem, no matter what present you're in—from its previous golden age—it's always a perfect past, at sufficient temporal distance from the present to prevent any close

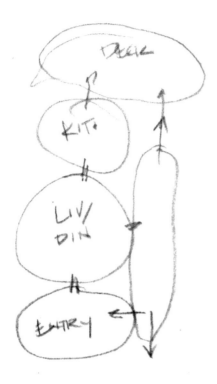

FIGURE 2.6 Bubbles of function should never be confused for rooms.

scrutiny—is due to an abandonment of first principles, which inevitably pertain to the relationship between how a building looks and what it does. Here is Greenough's lament, feel free to insert your own ideal and degenerate periods:

> If we trace architecture from its perfection in the days of Pericles to its manifest decay in the reign of Constantine, we shall find that one of the surest symptoms of decline was the adoption of admired forms and models for purposes not contemplated in their invention.[31]

He goes on to say that once these principles were abandoned we were left with nothing but "novelty, economy, and vainglory,"[32] and before long cats and dogs are living together. The first marks, the first graphemes, then, already come loaded with propositional content that veers toward either form or function, and therefore also with values that anchor the architecture to follow in an ethical relation to its purpose. That's a lot of weight for a few lines to carry.

Meanwhile, back at Petra's desk… There's something a bit claustrophobic about this reflective conversation between professor and student. Quist is making up the morphemes and graphemes, the words and lines, and he's also supplying the definitions, like a toddler who insists that his words and scribbles mean what he wants them to mean. He and Petra have circumscribed a tight little semantic world for themselves. This is necessary for the situation, which is the education of an architect, but as she continues to learn and develop her own internal conversation, Petra may mimic Quist's instructions in her own mind or test them on another student, and in so doing, more deeply engrave the vocabulary into her process. Again, that's just fine and necessary, as long as that pair of design languages, words and marks, remains situated in its context. When Petra goes home for winter break though, she will have a very hard time explaining to her mother exactly what she is learning and how she is learning it. To talk to her mother about the design process, the code-switching she is learning won't work, unless her mother "speaks" the design languages. Instead, she'll have to style-shift and adjust her linguistic register. She won't put it that way, of course; first, she'll roll her eyes… Mom, you just don't understand.

Petra is learning how to design while at the same time she is also receiving language instruction, so code-switching is still difficult for her, and she will continue to rely on the crutch of natural language. At desk crits she will talk her way into and out of problems; hundreds of words will fill the space where one drawing should be. On the other hand, Quist, like so many mature architects, probably has greater fluency in the language of drawing. That's why he's stuck with all those dychtics; he can't come up with any suitable nouns. Dychtic utterances demand supplementary information; "this" and "that" mean nothing without a gesture, a companion mark, or scribble. Her dominant language is still words; his, lines and marks. But they are both exercising a necessary occupational skill, the one, in fact, that determines professional competence and readiness to practice architecture.

Competence and readiness to practice are necessary but not suffi-cient for professional success, so let's dig a little bit deeper into the theory of linguistic register as an essential partner in the rhetoric of drawing. Different audi-ences require different speech. Mastery of the code switch between natural and graphic languages is an explicit goal of design education, although it may not be expressed exactly like that. Receiving far less attention, however, is the acquisi-tion of style-shifting skills. In short, code-switching occurs *between* languages; style-shifting happens *within* a language. It is a shift in tone, accent, vocabulary, or pronunciation. Put more plainly: we talk differently depending on to whom we are talking.

Style-shifting is a technique of pure persuasion. It's a tool for tuning your modes of speaking to different audiences and it requires an incisive understanding of those audiences. Politicians are chronic style-shifters, as one might expect in the realm of political rhetoric, but the best of them make it seem natural. Both Bill Clinton and George W. Bush benefitted from New England educations but upon embarking on their political careers each demonstrated mastery of the rhetori-cal power of the dropped "-g," or the useful second person plural "y'all," both of which are signifiers of regular-guy-ness. Nothing knocks the granite edges off an Ivy League education quite like a few strategically deployed y'alls. Of course, I'm not sayin' anything here that y'all don't already know.

Martin Joos first articulated the theory of linguistic register in a quirky lit-tle book called *The Five Clocks*. Because it is far from obvious why his book would have that title, he opens with a joke: "Ballyhough railway station has two clocks which disagree by some six minutes. When one helpful Englishman pointed the fact out to a porter, his reply was 'Faith, sir, if they was to tell the same time, why would we be having two of them?' " That's funny on so many different lev-els, but trying to explain a joke undermines its linguistic register, which oper-ates best without any tedious exegesis. What is linguistic register? According to Joos, it is the act of adapting—registering—one's language to the professional/audience situation. This was a radical idea when Joos published his theory in the 1960s, because it overturned the paradigm of a single "proper" language that people either mastered or didn't. Thus the joke about the clocks—okay, I'm explaining it—which is funny because it undermines the idea of one correct time. We need multiple clocks because not all times are the right time, all the time. Sociolinguistics as a field asserts that language itself adjusts to situations, rather than maintaining a universal standard. We adjust our speech and language—sometimes intentionally sometimes subconsciously—in order to distance or con-nect, exclude or include.

Joos identified five registers—intimate, casual, consultative, formal, and frozen—which calibrate our speech and language to different groups. The intimate register is (or should be) used only among family and friends; it may also include words and expressions known only to that group. Think of how you and your sister can exchange just a few key words to summon an entire family drama. Or how spouses or romantic partners can communicate in their own shorthand, with codes phrases, and nicknames that might be cringe-worthy to outside ears. The casual register consists of the informal language that is known and used in a defined social group—such as architects. The chatter at an AIA function, a reception at a school, design conversations among the staff at the office, are all in the casual register. Participants need not continually supply backstory or define terms; if you are part of the conversation, you have been initiated. The drawings that accompany these natural language conversations are also in the graphic version of the casual register. They might be gestural sketches; they might be on unlabeled and undated pieces of paper; their file names might indicate "in progress" or even more forceful disclaimers such as "not for distribution." What's said and drawn in the huddle room stays in the huddle room. Even though the group of designers may have different positions of authority, from intern to principal, the casual register is a leveler of conversation.

The consultative register is explicitly hierarchical, used from expert to non-expert, architect to citizen group, mentor to protégé, boss to intern, Quist to Petra, me to you. Notice, however, that I'm using contractions and the first person. Those are signifiers of casualness, so Microsoft Word keeps warning me not to use them. Yet I persist because I'm intentionally style-shifting out of my professorial consultative register and dressing down—style-shifting presents vividly in fashion—in order to ingratiate myself to you, my patient reader.[33] The consultative register both expects and welcomes the participation of the listener—relying on confirming utterances of "uh huh," "I see," "yes, okay," "right," so long as the listener knows her place. Not only words and drawings, but actions too can have register. In a design meeting, whether internal to an architect's office, with a client, or in public, the act of unrolling yellow trace paper is a consultative gesture. It is also an invitation: "by unrolling this paper we invite you to participate..." Participation is effected with just a little encouragement, some additional tools—pencils for everyone—and good faith on the part of all participants. Pull back from the unrolling in your imagination: the space where this happens has to support this consultative gesture as different spaces must support the casual. Two chairs side-by-side telegraph a different relationship than two chairs on either side of a desk. A table space capable of hosting a roll of trace paper communicates a very different type of invitation than rows of chairs facing a lectern and screen—especially if the room is darkened. It may seem like a small difference, but because space is itself part of the language of design, the setting, the context, the situation—all these carry illocutionary force, that is they convey supplemental messages, which can reinforce and augment or, if not well managed, undermine the speaker's message. The design of places, then, is both means and end.

The lectern and the screen set the stage for the formal register, which is the style for technical language directed at strangers. Architects and academics have multiple formal registers, and mixing them up can get us into trouble. Says Joos: "Describing formal style by departure from consultative style, the crucial difference is that participation drops out."[34] If participation "drops out" in a situation where participation is the only reason for attending, then what we have here, as the saying goes, is a failure to communicate. (We'll see that in action in Chapter 6.) Joos continues to explain that there might be other reasons why a speaker dons the formal register: "Non-participation is also enforced whenever a speaker is entirely uncertain of the prospective response."[35] In other words, the formal register serves as a shield to deflect any too-probing or unexpectedly hostile questions. Furthermore, the absence of participation

> infects the speaker also. He may speak as if he were not present, avoiding such allusions to his own existence as "I, me, mine" with the possible exception of "one"—a formal code-label—or "myself" in desperate situations. The speaker protects both the text and himself from involvement; presumably he will be absent if the roof collapses.[36]

In an architectural presentation, this disassociation might result in the drawings or the building playing the part of the speaker, as in "the elevation shows"; or retreating to the passive voice, as in "the site plan is drawn to..." One does expect—see, I just slipped into the formal register—that the material should match the register of the speech and situation; thus, in such a presentation, the architect would be clicking through near-final plans and renderings, not rolling out the paper seeking input.

The final register, what Joos calls "frozen" is ritualistic, appropriate for ceremonial, legal, or religious settings. It is rare and only marginally relevant to architectural situations, except perhaps some groundbreakings and dedications, and any document the preparation of which involves lawyers. In that sense, the "contract documents," that is, the drawings and narratives that establish the conditions of fulfillment of an architectural project are drafted in the frozen register. There will be more to say on that when we discuss wishes and instructions in Chapter 5.

Why do architects draw? Because much of what they have to communicate cannot be expressed in words. Yet in drawings as in language, there is a risk of focusing on the art of saying at the expense of what is being said: latent suspicions of ornamented speech, of rhetoric, translate easily to suspicions of the beautiful deception of visualizations, which are made more risky and facile with digital technologies. As Paul Ricoeur puts it, "It is always possible for the art of 'saying it well' to lay aside all concern for 'speaking the truth.'"[37] Design drawings, however, can't be described as true or false; they are more like fiction, or something not yet but potentially true. Because they have a unique relationship to reality, we should take a critically reflective look at how both our natural and our graphic languages persuade, and consider that they may sometimes be operating at cross-purposes.

NOTES

1. Zumthor, *Thinking Architecture*, P 10.
2. Bachelard, *Poetics of Space*, P 15. Whenever I read Bachelard's phrase "dream-memory" Neil Young's lyrics for "Helpless" come to mind: "with dream comfort memory to spare." Neil is quite the phenomenologist.
3. Ibid, P 14.
4. Ibid, P 15.
5. That phrase is itself a bit of rhetoric, which conflates the two nouns, "house" the physical building and "home" the social construct.
6. Why the present perfect tense? Because digital renderings have changed the representation game, which we will discuss in Chapter 7, and the way things have been in the past isn't necessarily how they are now.
7. Or, to be fair, all kinds of designers and planners and world-makers, but, I'm an architect, and so that's whom I'm writing about here. Don't take offense; think of it as synecdoche.
8. Ibid, P 12.
9. Goodman, *Languages of Art*, introduces the autographic/allographic distinction in Chapter 3.
10. It is certainly true that more than one person can work on a poem or essay, and that there is a long tradition of artists' workshops to execute paintings or sculpture, but it isn't technically necessary. With any architecture beyond the tiniest shed, it is.
11. Aristotle, *Rhetoric*, Part 3.
12. Aristotle, *Rhetoric*, Part 5.
13. Consider—do we really have to go here?—the different public perceptions of President Obama and his successor, Trump. The Trump trope, as it were, was "plain speaking" rather than "lofty rhetoric." The body politic, or at least a sufficient part of it, became suspicious of Obama's oratorical craft and preferred the blunt, utterly artless utterances of Trump.
14. Aristotle, *Poetics*, P 16.
15. Robbins, P 41.
16. Ibid, P 42.
17. Ibid, P 42.
18. Aristotle, *Poetics*, P 41.
19. The "desk crit" is the primary mode of architectural instruction. The teacher, often called the critic, visits her students' desks one by one, sits at their side, and discusses their work. There's an element of the confessional to the posture and content—forgive me, critic, for I have sinned, I have neglected the structure—but without the comforting cloak of anonymity.

20. It's also a useful tool to put my hair up when it becomes too much of a frizzy nuisance. This is another way in which the simple pencil is more useful than the most sophisticated computer. Just try putting your hair up with an iPad....

21. Schön, *Reflective Practitioner*, Chapter 3. Schön claims that this protocol illustrates the design process in the profession of architecture, but it more accurately should be described as illustrating the process of design education. They are not the same thing at all. Dana Cuff's 1991 book *Architecture: the Story of Practice* more accurately describes the professional "conversation."

22. Schön, P 80.

23. Ibid, P 81.

24. Ibid, P 81.

25. Ibid, P 81.

26. That said, sometimes naïve observations about this can be surprisingly profound. On an interdisciplinary study abroad program an English major said to the lone art major, "how can you draw like that?" The art student responded, "I just do it. How can you write like that?" The ten year old son of my faculty colleagues offered, "It's no different; it's all lines. Words and drawings are all lines."

27. Legendary educator, and my mentor, Jaan Holt regularly told students "there are no lines in architecture."

28. My colleague Dr. Paul Emmons has plumbed the life story of dashed lines in far more detail than I can here. Anyone interested can seek out his numerous publications such as his 2004 "Demiurgic lines: line-making and the architectural imagination" in *The Journal of Architecture*.

29. Emmons, "The Cosmogony of Bubble Diagrams," P 420.

30. Greenough, Horatio. *Form and Function: Remarks on Art, Design, and Architecture*.

31. Greenough, P 54.

32. Ibid.

33. Joos's book is one long style-shift from beginning to end in form and content, and he too directly addresses his reader.

34. Joos, *The Five Clocks*, P 34.

35. Ibid, P 35.

36. Ibid, P 36. The latter phrase, which might strike the casual reader as weird, refers I assume to the story of the poet Simonides who was serendipitously called out of a banquet where he was reciting a poem and thus saved from death when the roof collapsed. Explaining this story any further would lead us into the wonderful world of spatialized memory, which Cicero claims is part of rhetoric. So, it's applicable here, but a little too far off track to warrant any more discussion.

37. Ricoeur, *The Rule of Metaphor: Multi-disciplinary studies of the creation of meaning in language*, P 10.

CHAPTER 3
DIRECTION OF FIT

How does this architecture thing, the relationship between architect and client, start? It begins as a conversation or, more accurately, several interlaced conversations—between architect and client, between words and images, and ultimately between the work and the world. These are bilingual conversations, in which natural language and graphic language together yield imperfect translations, productive misunderstandings, and sometimes entirely unpredictable meanings. As we discussed in the last chapter, learning to be an architect involves learning this new graphic language—the language of drawing, with its potent powers of persuasion—and discovering that there is nothing natural about it. The conversation between professor and student code-switches between the natural and un-natural languages and in so doing models the code-switching mastery required of a design professional. There's far more to it than that, of course, not the least of which is the challenge of style-shifting or register-shifting, which we introduced in the last chapter. In this chapter, we'll start to dive deeper into the mechanics of language(s) and borrow shamelessly from grammar to sort through the different roles that architectural drawings play in these conversations. We'll start with a tale of two clients, each of whom opens the architectural conversation in a different way.[1]

In my few years in architectural practice, I worked for several tiny firms and one very large firm. Once I became a full-time educator, I had the luxury to describe myself as a "sole practitioner," meaning that I need not depend on a stream of clients walking in the door to pay my bills but I could take on a project if one walked into my life. (I could have just as accurately described myself as a freelance writer, meaning that no one was paying me to write anything; but if someone did, I would.) As a novice architect, I was always fascinated by the exchange of information between architect and client, particularly when things were going badly. As an educator, I am fascinated by the conversation between teacher and student, as I described in the previous chapter, and for the same reasons. To paraphrase the nursery rhyme, when things go well they go very, very well, and when they go bad, they're awful. The path to a building, like the one to the underworld, is paved with good intentions; everyone involved wants a good result, yet that path is full of detours, potholes, and misdirections. The interesting part is how those intentions are expressed and communicated. It's a language issue.

About ten years into my teaching career, I ended up with a client. We'll call him M. He was part of the neighborhood, running a small business frequented by many faculty and students. As one of the regular patrons, I had gotten to know him and we had chatted about life, the universe, and architecture over the years. When he finally decided to move out of a nearby attic—how Bachelardian!—he began to share his house-hunting travails with me. I accompanied him on one of these expeditions, riding along in the car with him and his real estate agent because he wanted my opinion of the various houses we saw. After a long process of house-dating he finally committed to a quirky older house a short walk from his shop and he asked me to come see it soon after he had moved in. He met me at the door and confessed that he wasn't comfortable in his own home; in fact he hadn't unpacked his boxes because he felt so alienated from it. He thought that maybe he needed architectural help, which is usually cheaper than psychological help.

This project did not involve a clever cocktail napkin *parti* sketch, nor did it require a complex bubble diagram to sort out functional relationships. The house already existed and was more than large enough for him, so the form/function problematic—mashing functions into a cool shape or wrapping something interesting around a rational functional arrangement—was already somewhat settled. So what was the problem? The house, in his view, didn't make a place for him and his life; it resisted his advances. Where does the architectural conversation begin in this case? With a quirky list of things that he needed the house to do for him. My field notes (see Figure 3.1) from one of our initial meetings shows a list under the title "program" of the following things that needed to be accommodated on the first floor:

Your keys
Someone else's keys
Today's mail
Yesterday's mail that you haven't opened
A post-it note with a phone number but no name
The yard guy's card
The plumber's card
Spare change
A pebble
Stamps
Gimme hats
Gloves that don't belong to you
Coats
Feathers

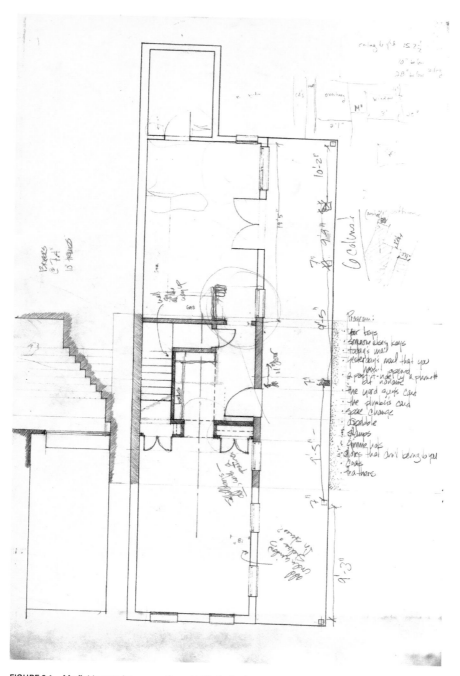

FIGURE 3.1   My field notes from a meeting with M; the list is as close as we got to an architectural program.

The house occupied a double-lot, was two stories tall, with no basement. M envisioned the first floor as a social space with easy access to its long side porch and the yard, which also needed some design attention. The second floor, however, needed to be clearly private. The program list for that floor (see Figure 3.2) was:

Private is private
Sneaky access
Architectural mystery…who goes there?
Nancy Drew and the 99 Steps[2]
CDs and stereo

There was no need in this project to make a list of conventional rooms—master bedroom, bath, living room, kitchen, and so on. The house already had those and there was no need for more space. The problems weren't with the house *qua* house; it had everything necessary to be a house. What it lacked were those things that were necessary to make it a *home*, those things least amenable to visualization. These inchoate wishes of his, then, were offered to me, the architect, in words, in natural language. Reading them now, these lists have a wistful poetry to them, an economy of words that evokes the quotidian rituals of dwelling. They don't, however, easily fit into an architectural hierarchy of major/minor, serving/served, nor do they offer an immediate tectonic image. Is there even an architectural answer to this question? Maybe M just needed a nice table and a coat rack. But that's not what I drew because at that point I was sure that the answer to every problem of building was a building.[3]

Before I answered his word-list with sketches—his natural language with my graphic language—I did a set of drawings of the building as it was, what architects call the "existing conditions" (see Figure 3.3). In every project, the drawings of the existing conditions set the terms of reality, the set of agreed-upon facts, without which any succeeding conversation is nonsense. These drawings are never correct the first time; reality is elusive that way. In this drawing, you can see at least three layers of information. The base drawing is a photocopy of the original drafted plan, based on some long-lost freehand survey I had probably done on graph paper on a clipboard. Drawn in red are things I needed to find out, whether dimensions or conditions. There are pencil marks from a final site visit, stringing together dimensions, correcting things I got wrong the first time around, or filling in missing information. This drawing documents my interrogative conversation with the situation as I wrestled with a three-dimensional piece of the physical world, where nothing seemed straight—neither plumb nor level—in order to flatten it into a two-dimensional representation that I could drag back to my desk. This kind of drawing has a particular relation to the world: it claims to match it.

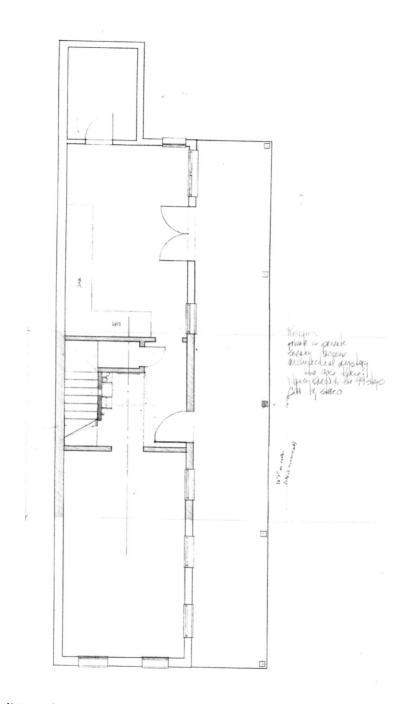

FIGURE 3.2   Not as much was needed on the second floor except for mystery and privacy.

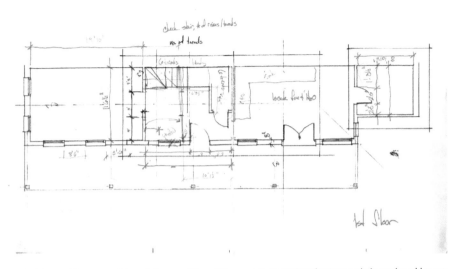

FIGURE 3.3   My survey of the existing conditions. It is surprisingly challenging to smash the real world accurately into a drawing.

Now let's imagine another client—we'll call her K—who is dissatisfied with her domestic environment but is less verbal and more visual than M. Space is her problem; she has a hunch that she needs more of it, that her house is too tight. Her kitchen is cluttered, her home office a junk room. The Container Store can no longer contain her. She can't seem to corral her image of how she *should* be living into alignment with how she actually *is* living. "I need more space..." she mutters to herself every time she opens her closet, pushes a pile of books to the side, or bumps into her table. At some point, when the self-help clutter mavens have failed to solve her problem, she decides to hire an architect to design an addition for her house. She has been thinking about this for a long time, as her Pinterest followers know, and she carries a folder full of images to her first meeting with the architect. These pages, torn or downloaded from the so-called "shelter publications," show what she wants her renovated and expanded house to look like. There's a generous indoor/outdoor kitchen from some ranch in Arizona, a retro-chic master bath from a Manhattan condo, and a high-ceilinged family room opening to a redwood deck with a view of the San Francisco Bay. K lives in suburban Maryland, a place with four moist seasons, and she has a view to her neighbor's backyard, yet she suffers no cognitive dissonance from this patchwork house. Her rational mind knows there is no place in the space/time continuum where this house could actually exist as a montage of these disparate sources. This place-quilt can only exist in her imagination, yet she wants it all nonetheless.

Neither a poet nor a philosopher, she knows that this scrapbook of aspirations is as close as she can come to expressing her wishes. Words for this client-in-the-making aren't sufficient.

This moment is as fraught with crushing disappointment as carrying Jennifer Anniston's picture to the hair stylist, but it is the best way for K to effect an image transplant of what is in her own head into the architect's. She could, like M, write down lists of things, attributes, qualities, and quantities. She could try to describe in words what she is imagining but that seems to be a step backward for her, because her imaginings are already visual. So she has searched for images that approximately match the ones in her mind, correctly intuiting that for this crucial first exchange with her architect an image-to-image translation is more efficient than word-to-image, even if a boatload of potentially irrelevant or even contradictory information comes along for the ride. In fact, the images she carries in her folder bear too much information. These *extrania* in the photographs are just as real as the longed-for bleached wood floor and Venetian plaster, but she's quite capable of selective blindness, so she ignores the red leather couch, the lounging dog, the stack of purple towels. She has deleted them in her mind. There are as many red herrings in these images as there are true clues, because that is the driftnet nature of photographs.

When philosopher Gilbert Ryle says that "language is our only access to the mind of another,"[4] we might think he means natural language, like my conversations with M, and the lists of performance criteria for his house. But these source images carefully collected by K constitute a different kind of language, one that is visual rather than verbal. As language, these images also have a particular kind of force. They communicate in a particular mode: they beseech, plead, and entreat. In this respect they are not unlike one interpretation of the bison cave drawings: a wish for what is illustrated to materialize. The photo of the Arizona kitchen, handed to the architect, speaks for the client, saying, "Would that my kitchen were this way...may some of these characteristics find a home in my kitchen...if my kitchen were like this..." This kind of image too, has a particular relation to the world: it wishes for the world to match it.

The architect listens, visits the site, takes notes, inventories and measures some things, begins to make drawings of the existing conditions, and takes photographs.[5] In each of these actions, the architect is harvesting information from the world, then retreating to the studio to translate the client's wishes for the finishes and space. The architect has to play detective, to figure out how the client got to this point. The client's opening request—"I need more space"—may not even be an accurate statement of the problem; the obvious answers are not always the correct ones. Maybe she needs better space, maybe different space, but the client's mind isn't tuned to discern the differences among "more," "better," and "different." It is a big step for someone to decide to have a portion of her own world remade, to engage someone to rearrange time, space, and matter into a future condition from which there is no retreat. While the world is full of house additions, *this* addition, on *this* house has never been designed nor made, nor will it ever be again. So K tries to describe through images a wish for something that doesn't exist, while the architect tries to shape the client's words and wish-images into a thing that might. The architect looks for the alignments and misalignments among what the client says, shows, and lives, as if filming a scene from three camera angles. She hasn't yet begun the design process, but the architect already stands in a chain of translations, the products of which will eventually form the links for another chain of translations between these wishes and the world.

This exchange of wishes between client and architect is the beginning of a discourse occurring in different languages. It isn't symmetrical, however; as we've discussed, the degrees of fluency are quite different on each side. As Ed Robbins explains in *Why Architects Draw*, "While drawing has been a crucial mode of discourse within architecture and a central part of architectural education for centuries, the same cannot be said of the role of drawing in society in general."[6] Words and images go back and forth; sometimes client's words are answered with architect's images, as with M, sometimes vice versa. Sometimes the answers come back in the same language, words for words and images for images. Whatever the language(s) in this beginning phase, it is an *optative* discourse, an exchange of wishes for a future that could be made real. That last part—that the wishes *could* be made real—is what sets such discourse apart from a game of fantasy, or idle wishing. Moreover, the credibility of that reality is established in the documentation of the existing conditions. As Robbins explains, "Discourse, in this sense, is the movement to and fro of messages among a number of individuals or groups and the act by which understanding passes from premises to consequences."[7]

To work from premises—the site, the existing conditions, the client's wishes, the budget—to consequences—a design proposal—the architect follows the normative procedures of professional practice.[8] She prepares a set of drawings, and perhaps a physical model, of the existing conditions. Then she meets with the client, after which she produces sketches (see Figure 3.4), then schematic drawings and, again, perhaps a model, physical or digital. She then moves on to the design development phase, where elements and materials are named and dimensioned. When both client and architect have agreed to these decisions, she commences the production of construction documents, which include drawings, schedules, and a hefty stack of words known as "the specifications." The construction documents indicate exactly what and where—they *specify*, obviously—but they leave much of the how to the contractor. Depending on the contract, there may be a "pricing set" from which bids are solicited prior to the completion of the construction documents. Each step is followed by meetings with the client where, as Robbins describes, "the drawing(s) serves as both the subject of conversation and the object of our endeavors."[9] Such meetings, Robbins continues, "always involve verbal communication with the drawings serving to direct, order, clarify,

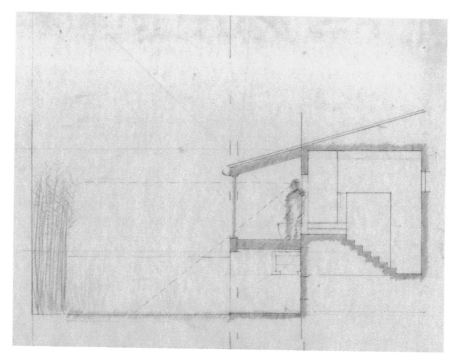

FIGURE 3.4 A sketched section that begins to imagine how things might be, and what one might see from the mystery-filled second floor.

and record ideas that come out of the conversation."[10] Once this design process has begun, the drawings—both subject and object—issue from the architect. The verbal communication is a game of speaking and listening, while the visual communication is a game of representing and seeing, in a multi-sensory conversation.

During construction, the architect visits the site (what exactly she does there is the subject of much wordsmithing in contracts) and thus concludes the construction administration phase, during which time the project is built in tidy accordance with the documents, to the happily-ever-after satisfaction of the client, the pride of the architect, and the profit of the contractor. Or so the story goes... The comedy of errors[11] that is design and construction is simply systemically fraught because of the many languages in which its content must be communicated and the wildly different levels of proficiencies that its practitioners and audiences possess. It's no surprise that the Babel myth originated at a construction site.

This is *construction*, the defining act of architecture, or as historian Robin Evans put it, the translation of drawing to building, of wish to reality. The reality, however, is rarely—perhaps never—the clean, organized sequence I've just summarized. Between each step there are crevasses of problems—foreseen and unforeseen—disagreements, and misunderstandings among the myriad participants of the design and building process. Furthermore, it isn't only one act of translation, as Evans so eloquently described it in his seminal work, *Translations from Drawing to Building and Other Essays*, but rather a rolling and nested sequence of translations. From the client's opening words and scrapbook of images to the call and response of requests for information during construction, these serial and simultaneous translations in aggregate affect the intended relation between the drawings and the world, which is a *seamless fidelity.* This is one of the creation myths of architecture, that the wish of the client impregnates the mind of the architect,[12] whose charge, then, is to give birth to the building, ensuring "…maximum preservation in which both meaning and likeness are transported from idea through drawing to building with minimum loss. This is the doctrine of essentialism."[13] The translation from drawing to building, however, follows other earlier translations, as we have seen; there are other from/to relations. Think of this visually (see Figure 3.5): the from/to can be diagrammed with the two conditions separated by a space. An arrow in that space sets the from/to, showing which one is where you are and which is the destination. For the existing conditions, the arrow points *from* the world *to* the drawing. At the point of the construction documents, the arrow points to the world, *from* drawing *to* building. What is going on between those moments to switch the arrow's direction? Design.

Semanticists and communications theorists will tell you that every utterance—the unpoetic but precise word favored in such writing—establishes a relation to the world. If we interpret "utterance" as broadly as possible, then all manner of representations rendered in words, spoken or written, images, codes, numbers, and other notations, establish relations to the world.[14] The question, then, is this: what relation to the world do you intend with this—this drawing, this diagram, this model? The images that our space-constrained client shows her architect intend one kind of relation; the drawings the architect makes of the existing conditions, another; the design drawings that follow, another still. Architects learn in their required professional practice classes that a project has specific phases, each with different kinds of drawings.[15] I'm suggesting, however, that there are really only two categories of architectural drawings and they are defined by the relation they establish with the world: there are drawings that intend to match the world and there are drawings that intend for the world to match them. To explain this, we need to slip out of the world of images and into the world of words to talk about grammar.

The first responsibility of language is to establish the speaker's relation to the world; nothing makes sense without that. The part of speech capable of

FIGURE 3.5 Design has the power to change the arrow's direction.

establishing that relation is the amazing verb. Without verbs, speech would be a litany of names and attributes without context, agency, or time. We don't care about dog and man until biting is involved, and then we want to know who is biting whom. Verbs come in various tenses, modes, and voices. The voice, active or passive, indicates whether the subject of the verb is acting or being acted upon, biting or being bitten. The passive voice, all too familiar in political dissimulation, is subjectless.[16] Legal counsel has advised legions of venal politicians to say "mistakes were made" as a way to admit the obvious while dodging the responsibility. The not-so-subtext is that, yes, there were mistakes, but it was certainly not I, the speaker, who made them. The active-voice version of that sentence is as rare as a centaur: I made mistakes. More common are its conjugations: You made mistakes. S/he made mistakes. We made mistakes. Y'all[17] made mistakes. They made mistakes. The awkward passive voice flags a desperate attempt to distance the self-conscious "I" from its mistake-making relation to the world. Whether passive or active, these are declarations, assertions of fact. They can be debated, rejected, or disproved, *because* they are statements of facts. *You* made mistakes, but *I* did not. Without getting too alethiological about it, statements of facts are either truths or lies.

There could be a world, however, where mistakes might or might not have been made, where someone is pondering mistake-making, weighing the "what-ifs." If we want to wonder, rather than accuse, we need to change the mode of the expression from a declaration to something else entirely. If a mistake be made... Would that no mistakes had been made... Had mistakes not been made, then...then what? Then entire new narratives arise and the completion of sentences becomes a choice among possibilities. Things might have been different, other than the way they are. And with that thought our imaginations are liberated from the linear slog of the present timeline to contemplate possible other worlds and, of course, possible other mistakes. The liberation from declaration is the job of the subjunctive mode.

When we speak or write we use the same words to describe the real, the potentially real, the unlikely, and the impossible, all with equal clarity. That any listener/reader can tell the difference depends on our distinguishing the mood, or mode, of the words, reflecting "the speaker's view of the ontological character of an event" which may be "real or unreal, certain or possible, wished or demanded."[18] To say "There was a centaur in my parking space" is to make a grammatically correct sentence, but one with a dubious relation to reality. The listener has to know which of those terms has a referent in the real world to evaluate the sentence's descriptive truth.[19] To say "If there were a centaur in my parking space, I would immediately call the tow truck" is entirely different. Note the change in the verb form from "was" to "were." That indicates the mode,[20] which is revealed in the positions and inflections of the verbs and their auxiliaries.

To oversimplify a long-running linguistic debate, there are three verb modes in Indo-European languages, the big linguistic family that includes English.

The modes generally agreed upon are the indicative, the imperative, and the subjunctive. Through the natural—at least for most speakers—uses of these verb forms we establish the relation between what we are saying and the situation. The indicative, which describes factual or neutral situations, derives from the Latin *indicere*, meaning "to point out, to make known." Indicative statements include remarks about the world, such as "this wall is concrete," or about conditions, whether in the past, as in "I made a mistake," or the present, "I am hungry." Formally, there is a future indicative but it's a prediction, not a description, so we are not going to talk about it. (That sentence is in the future indicative, thus we did just talk about it.) An indicative statement can be argued about, verified, or contested. There's always a possible counter to an indicative statement, such as the juvenile "is not!" which only invites the equally juvenile rejoinder "is so!" Indicative statements don't only describe the banal or the obvious, as I'm doing here. "All men are created equal" is an indicative statement, the truth of which has been subjected to generations of exegeses as its underlying referents have gradually evolved. An indicative statement may be grammatically simple, but that in no way implies that its content is simple.

We spend a lot of our daily words just describing things and situations, particularly now that our ubiquitous communication devices have made narrating our lives so easy. "I'm at the corner." "We're all waiting for you." Occasionally, we have to say, "Get over here now." Our second mode, the imperative, conveys an order. Like "indicative," the word "imperative" derives from the Latin, in this case *imperare*, which means "to impose or to command." When I whine, indicatively, "I'm hungry," I can then blurt, imperatively, "Send me a cheeseburger and a new *Rolling Stone*."[21] Interestingly, the imperative is characterized by the lack of an articulated subject, but it is always understood to be directed at the second person. In other words, there has to be someone on the receiving end of an imperative, but she need not be named. The "hey, you" is implied. An imperative carries the expectation of compliance. While an indicative can be debated, any response to an imperative that isn't "yessir" is considered back talk, a frustrating situation familiar to all current and former children. Imperatives are acceptable only in limited social settings where rank, obedience, and action are understood and mutually agreed upon, such as the military and professional football.

And now we get to the really interesting mode, the subjunctive. There is some argument, among people who argue about such things, over the existence of the subjunctive in modern English, but the disagreement centers on a formal question rather than a semantic one. No linguist proposes that the English language is incapable of expressing subjunctive thoughts, only that the verb itself is not formally inflected and depends instead on what are called "modal auxiliaries," or extra words.[22] The word also derives, of course, from Latin: *subjungere*, meaning "to harness, to yoke together, to join below." The subjunctive, then, conveys an indeterminate set of intentions and wishes that are linked in a loose chain of possibility. The familiar folk song "If I Had a Hammer..." is a long, subjunctive rumination on a series of conditions contrary to fact, spelling out what the singer would do with various objects if he had them. To return to my declaration of hunger and my demand for a cheeseburger, I can temper my whining and rudeness through subjunctivity: "Boy, do I wish I had a cheeseburger." There's the poignant, though archaic "Would that I had a cheeseburger!" There are also different subspecies of subjunctive, some of which might at first sound imperative: "I require that you bring me a cheeseburger." Or "The person nearest the grill shall bring me a cheeseburger." This curious ambiguity will be addressed later, but for now, note the use of "shall" with the third person; that wording will sound quite familiar to architects and contractors.

Thanks to our Latin etymology, the names of the first two modes, the indicative and the imperative, are transparent to their use. They are what they do. But the word "subjunctive," with its meaning of harnessing or joining together, is stubbornly opaque. What is being harnessed? What is being joined? According to linguists, humans once expressed ideas simply, in sequential, independent clauses called "coordinate" clauses because they were ordered equally to one another.[23] The relation of one thought to another was inferred by adjacency. The familiar Miranda warning is an example of this: "You have the right to remain silent. Anything you say can and will be used against you." As languages gradually evolved they developed the capacity to express more complex thoughts in sentences constructed of a main clause plus a dependent, sub-ordinate, i.e. ordered hierarchically one below another, clause. A subordinate rewrite of the Miranda warning might yield "You have the right to remain silent, as your words can and will be used against you." Or: "Because your words can and will be used against you, you have the right to remain silent." Thus the subjunctive is the mode/mood/manner of joining or harnessing two previously independent clauses together to form a more complex sentence and to establish the relationship between the clauses. As the separate and equal coordinated independent clauses acquire hierarchy and dependency upon one another, they develop the conditional and contextually construed relation characteristic of the subjunctive. The subjunctive whole of the two clauses is greater and more interesting than the sum of their harnessing.

What the subjunctive does through this harnessing and joining of meaning is to expand vastly the expressive range of the same kit of word parts, letting us imagine conditions contrary to fact, wishes which may or may not be fulfilled, demands and proposals—basically a "variety of deontic meanings."[24] Each of these inhabits its own little subjunctive sub-world: there are the volitive, or optative, which describes the pleading and beseeching of the client or the bison-painter; the jussive, or mandative, first cousins to the imperative; and the conditional subjunctives, of the "if/then" variety, to name a few. The vast expressive range of the subjunctive continues to confound grammarians, as it seems to resist the kind of clear description available to the other modes, but it includes belief, hope, opinion, hypothesis, wish, possibility, probability, preference, doubt, imagination, fear, need—all of which sound a lot like design.[25] The subjunctive in many languages manifests itself in the actual form of the verb, or in its ending, as in Latin, but more often than not, in English, it uses modal auxiliary words such as "that" and "if," which cast the thoughts that follow into the realm of the imagination. Radio listeners are familiar with one of the most common contemporary subjunctive phrases: "the following is [indicative] a test" "of the emergency broadcast system… *If this were [subjunctive] a real emergency* … " Together, we have a statement of fact—"is"—and a conditional—"if…were."

What do these three modes have to do with architectural drawing? As Francis James has written, "Mood signifies the intended relation between words and world, and context shows who intends the relation (usually the speaker)."[26] Architectural drawings establish a relation between lines/marks and world and, as with language, the mode signifies what that relation is. Even with the caveat that the division of words from world is a contrivance—the words are already in the world, as are the lines and the paper—this linguistic theory casts a new light on the communicative responsibilities of architectural drawing. It is the relation the architect intends between drawings and world, then, that sets the mode and thus the appropriate marks and media. We can diagram these three modes—indicative, subjunctive, imperative—in a triangle, giving each its specific corner, but the apparent equilateral relation among the modes has a geometric elegance that is as appealing in the abstract as it is misleading in actuality. A more accurate visual image might be an isosceles triangle, with the indicative sitting alone in factual satisfaction some distance from the base formed by the world-making bloc of the imperative and the subjunctive (see Figure 3.6).

This is not just an architect's wish for a clean visualization; the diagram allows us to sort out the full spectrum of architectural drawings as they position

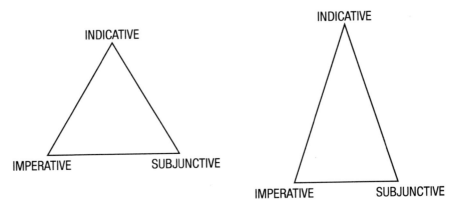

FIGURE 3.6   The relationship among the three modes is more isosceles than equilateral.

themselves relative to the world. On the indicative side are the drawings that match the world; on the other, the subjunctive and the imperative together desire to make the world match them. This image of shifting the modes out of their three-way equality and into an opposition of indicative against a subjunctive/imperative alliance is based on James' argument in *The Semantics of the English Subjunctive*. His opening analogy, conveniently, is an architectural drawing: "Consider, for example, an architect's sketch for a house he intends to build. He intends for the world to match his sketch, which is his 'blueprint.' "[27] The representation of this wish for the intended building both precedes and orders its possible fulfillment; it represents its own conditions of satisfaction. He continues,

> Now consider an artist's sketch of the house after it is built. He intends for the sketch, which is his 'record,' to match the world. The sketches may look exactly alike, but they differ in their manner of representation. If the same person had occasion to draw both kinds of sketches, he might choose to do 'blueprints' on blue paper and 'records' on yellow paper to help keep orderly files. The colors would then serve to signify the manner of representation.[28]

In other words, the drawings themselves represent intentionality, the "direction of fit" between world and work.[29]

Can we tell the direction of fit of a drawing such as this one by Otto Eggers, John Russell Pope's partner and master renderer (see Figure 3.7)? On the one hand, the precision, exquisite rendering of materials, and the inclusion of

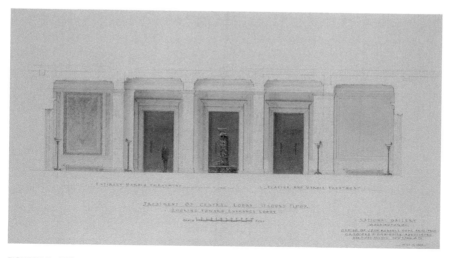

FIGURE 3.7   This 1939 drawing by Otto Eggers is titled "Treatment of Central Lobby Ground Floor Looking toward Entrance Lobby" for the National Gallery

light fixtures and a well-dressed human might lead us to believe that this is a doc-umentation of an existing place; the marble is rendered with such specificity that it must be drawn from the world. Look again, though, and there's something odd about how the bilateral symmetry of the doorway and panels is being undermined by the change of material on the far right. Fortunately, we have recourse to accom-panying text, loyal friend of the logocentric: one note reads, "entirely marble treat-ment," the other, "plaster and marble treatment." This drawing is directed toward the world, a subjunctive representation of two options in the same drawing. The drawing says, "*If it were* plaster and marble it would be thus; if it were entirely marble, thus." (Why is that guy standing there? Perhaps he's made his choice, and is wishing for the viewer to follow him.) The words "plaster or marble" alone would not have sufficed; what makes this such a persuasive drawing—a rhetori-cal utterance—is the profoundly convincing representations of the materials. The conditions of satisfaction are so clear that we, the viewers, can make an informed decision about the world we intend to make.

In his essay on drawing and building, Robin Evans reflects on the dif-ference between drawings that artists do and drawings that architects do. He remarks on the curious problem that architects face in drawing things that don't yet exist. James even uses the same terminology as Evans to separate the makers of these two types of drawings, architects, and artists. Despite all sorts of "ideal-ization, distortion, or transmogrification" as Evans puts it, the subject of an artist's work has for most of the history of art been taken from nature, from the world as it exists. Architecture, however, "is brought into existence through drawing. The subject matter (the building or space) will exist after the drawing, not before it."[30] Evans, however, passes over the translations that come before, the ones that provide the content for the drawings, as his interest is only the translations that follow from them. Where do the former come from? The world. Evans positions artists as the ones who represent that world and architects as the ones who bring a world into existence, yet architects actually occupy both positions. There are two directions of fit in architectural drawing, with two sets of arrows pointing between world and work. One side literally draws from the world; the other draws toward it.

These two directions of fit can occupy the same paper space. Eggers's drawing contains convincing bits of the real world (marble so convincing we would never take it for granite) embedded in the wishes to make them more persua-sive. Two other drawings by Eggers, one for the fountain in the Gallery's rotunda (see Figure 3.8) and one to study the Donatello Galleries (see Figure 3.9), also demonstrate this direction of fit chiasmus. In both of these studies the architec-tural wish is anchored by representations of real works of art. In the drawing for the fountain, one figure—the statue of Mercury—is drawn so masterfully that we would recognize its compliant if we were to see it. Gazing at the fountain is one of Eggers's well-dressed scale figures; a straight line runs from his eye and brushes the lip of the not-yet-real fountain on its way to the not-yet-real spouting water.

FIGURE 3.8   Eggers's "Fountain in the Rotunda," 1939.

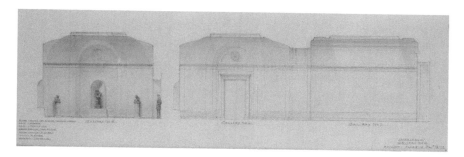

FIGURE 3.9   Eggers's 1939 study for the "Donatello Gallery 6 and 7."

This one drawing has several arrows, literal and metaphorical, pointing in and out of the real world, and our understanding of its relationship to the world depends on our ability to read the marks of intentionality. A real bronze of a fictional—as far as we know—god will balance on a not-yet-real basin, and a fictional future visitor will direct his gaze thus; he will see the water in motion, but not the water at rest. The line carries the intention of the view. The Donatello Gallery study includes drawings of the sculptor's works, casting real shadows across fictional surfaces, the materials of which are listed.

It isn't always obvious what is real and what is not, a dilemma we'll address in more depth later, particularly in images of such craft as these, and in contemporary digital renderings. It's not as simple as James's architect, who has his "blueprint" drawing depicting the building he imagines, and another yellow one of the building as-built. Today, this exchange of material from real to fictional includes photographically sampled bits of the real world—building materials, plants, and all sorts of entourage. They have all been harvested from other worlds and resettled in new possible environments; if the renderer isn't attentive, inconsistent shadows or light from the wrong direction can unmask them as interlopers in the fictional world.

To complicate matters even more, remember that architects make more things than drawings. Even Goodman throws in the metaphorical towel when he finally faces the problem that architectural documents pose for his grand unification theory of creative production: "The architect's papers are a curious mixture. The specifications are written in ordinary discursive verbal and numerical language. The renderings made to convey the appearance of the finished building are sketches. But what of the plans?"[31] Yeah, what of the plans? They are a curious mixture indeed, not only in their making but in to whom exactly they are directed in their world-matching ways. Moreover, the existence of the building is entirely dependent on a multitude of craftworkers and laborers who, until the moment of translation to building, had no role whatsoever in the drawings. Evans writes about this "peculiar disadvantage" that architects suffer because they do not work directly in the medium of the final work the way artists do, or can. In *Languages of Art*, Goodman wrestles with this issue but allows that it is not unique to architecture. As we mentioned in the second chapter, some creative production is, according to Goodman, "autographic," that is, the work of a sole author; some is "allographic," dependent on others for its fulfillment.[32] A poem is a good example of the former, a symphony of the latter. Or, to bring it back to the visual arts that Evans is talking about, painting is autographic and architecture is allographic, not only in the production of the building itself but the often the drawings, too. Many hands will touch a set of architectural drawings—whether physical or digital—adding to, changing, erasing/deleting, before the translation to building. Architectural documents—both depictions and descriptions, to borrow Goodman's terms—are means to another end but it is an oversimplification to say they are only that. They are our portal into the possible.

"Language," says Paul Ricoeur, "is itself the process by which private experience is made public."[33] In this case, the language is graphic: how does the image deeply inside our mind's eye become knowable to another being, shared? Remember, "drawing" is both verb and noun, an action and a thing (as is, interestingly, "talk)." The "curious mixture," as Goodman describes it, of words, numbers, diagrams, sketches, chatter, and gesture that bounces back and forth from the real to the possible is saturated with belief, hope, opinion, hypothesis, wish, possibility, probability, preference, doubt, imagination, fear, need. The following two chapters will take a closer look at the subspecies in each of these categories, first at a spectrum of indicative drawings and the myriad ways in which they can match some aspect of the world, then at wishes and instructions, the drawings that aim to change the world.

NOTES

1. One of these is a real individual client; the other is a composite of several I've known.
2. I think I must have added that myself.
3. To this day I have no idea what he saw in his mind's eye when he shared these wishes. We never discussed "style" or how things might look. Instead, we began a series of discussions that were more like therapy than design: I would ask him a few questions about how he and his house were getting along, make a few sketches that addressed where the problems seemed to be, and he would hand me an envelope full of cash. He preferred it that way. So this hardly qualifies as a correct story to illustrate the design process, but it does illuminate a few things—that our relationships with buildings, particularly those with which we are intimate, are complex and discursive.
4. Ryle, *The Concept of Mind*, P 15.
5. One "makes" drawings but "takes" photographs, because photography is a kind of theft. See Sontag, *On Photography*.
6. Robbins, *Why Architects Draw*, P 29.
7. Ibid.
8. What follows is a brief summary to get us to the main point. We'll take a more detailed look at the phases of design in Chapter 5.
9. Robbins, *Why Architects Draw*, P 3.
10. Ibid.
11. A comedy in the Shakespearean and Seinfeldian sense, that is, a story of human frailty, ambition, mistakes, and misunderstandings, but in which nobody dies.
12. Fifteenth-century architect Filarete describes the process:

    > Since no one can conceive by himself without a woman, by another simile, the building cannot be conceived by one man alone. As it cannot be done without a woman, so he who wishes to build needs an architect...When the architect has given birth, he becomes mother of the building.
    >
    > Book II, *Treatise on Architecture*.

13. Evans, *Translations from Drawing to Building and Other Essays*, P 181.
14. Aren't all these things, utterances included, already in the world? What is the human-made world, after all, if not a conglomeration of utterances in various media? Yes, the speaker and the spoken are always already in the world, but creative acts of production do expose the space between the one making the representations and the representations themselves. And it's that space, specifically, that demands our attention in the case of architectural representation.

15. More on this in Chapter 5…
16. I've used it liberally here, which provokes the AI grammar nanny in Microsoft Word to point it out to me disapprovingly each time. Yet I persist.
17. Or "you guys" depending on where you're from. English doesn't have a distinct second person plural, leaving it to regional convention.
18. www.britannica.com/topic/mood-grammar#ref285707 is the source of this quote, but the internet has explanations of mood to suit every level of grammar geekiness.
19. Nelson Goodman explains all this in exquisite detail in *Languages of Art*, often using centaurs as his example of a word with a null reference. Goodman fans will already have picked up on that little mythological homage.
20. These words, "mood" and "mode," are used interchangeably, as one is really just a corruption of the other. I prefer and will use "mode" because it retains more of its original meaning, "in the manner of," as opposed to the touchy-feely connotations of "mood."
21. Neil Young, "Crime in the City." It sounds better when he sings it.
22. An "inflected language" is one in which the ending of the word signifies its role in the sentence. Latin is solidly inflected; you can rearrange words to poetic effect and, as long as the correct endings cling to the words, the meaning is preserved. Not so with English.
23. There are several sources for the etymology of the subjunctive: Wayne Harsh, in his *The Subjunctive in English*, quotes on P 20 the 1862 *The Grammar of English Grammars* by Goold Brown.
24. Berk, L.M. *English Syntax: From Word to Discourse*, Oxford University Press, NY, 1999, P 149–50. "Deontic" means pertaining to duty, obligation, intention, and desire…and implies action.
25. Harsh's *The Subjunctive in English* has an extensive survey of opinions on the uses of the subjunctive; Paola Frascari provided me the list given here.
26. James, *Semantics of the English Subjunctive*, P 18.
27. James, *Semantics of the English Subjunctive*, P 12.
28. Ibid, P 12–13.
29.

> The expression 'conditions of satisfaction' has the usual process-product ambiguity as between the *requirement* and the *thing required*…the key to understanding representation is conditions of satisfaction. Every intentional state with a direction of fit is a representation of its conditions of satisfaction.
>
> Searle, *Intentionality*, P 13.

30. Evans, *Translations from Drawing to Building and Other Essays*, P 165.
31. Goodman, *Languages of Art*, P 218. He's falling into the habit that non-architects have of calling the set of orthographic drawings "plans," when in fact plans are only one kind of architectural drawing.
32. Goodman, *Languages*, P 113.
33. Ricoeur, *Interpretation Theory*, P 19.

CHAPTER 4
MATCHING THE WORLD

Architecture begins and ends in pictures.

Robin Evans, *The Projective Cast*

"Wow, that looks just like..."

That's the usual praise for a drawing that matches the world well, a portrait that looks like its subject, or a flower or tree faithful enough to its subject that the species can be identified. As a child, I spent hours drawing the world and, thanks to my late mother's archival tendencies, I have all of my drawings of the world I inhabited, through the eyes I had, in the childish hand that struggled to match the world as well as my mother's did.

She was an artist, a painter, but she was first a drawer, which in this case means one who draws, not a place for socks. It may be an odd deployment of a familiar word, but I use it because "draftsperson" sounds too mechanical, and "draughtsperson" too pretentious. She didn't break any artistic boundaries, nor was she interested in questioning the relationship between drawing and the world. For her, paintings or drawings were always *of* something. Their success, in her critical eyes, depended on fidelity to the subject. And she was just as critical of my drawings; even as a child I remember her pointing out with gentle frankness one or another part of a drawing that wasn't correct. When one is matching the world, things are either correct or incorrect. Linguists would say such drawings, analogous to utterances, have "truth conditions." Is that or is that not the Glen Ridge Women's Club (see Figures 4.1 and 4.2)?

Why do we make such drawings? My mother painted portraits of people and their houses on commission but often she just chose a house or a place that she simply liked. By drawing the Glen Ridge Women's Club, she made it her own. Her drawing has what Nelson Goodman calls a "compliant" and, as a representation, it *depicts* rather than *denotes*. In my life now, her drawing is more real than its

FIGURE 4.1   My father photographed the Glen Ridge Women's Club so my mother could refer to it while drawing off-site at home. Drawing by Dorathy B. Piedmont

compliant, and it represents—though it does not depict—my mother, more than it represents a building on Ridgewood Avenue. She drew and painted to remember, which is also why we take photographs, but drawings and paintings are very different kinds of rememberings from photographs. When we turn our attention to something, pencil in hand and blank sheet on lap, we face the unfathomable complexity of reality and we have to select what to draw. There is no way to draw it all. By contrast, when we raise a camera—or, now, a phone—to our eyes we may

FIGURE 4.2   My mother's drawing, which we can check for truth conditions against the photograph. Photo by J. Donlan Piedmont

shift the frame, or tune the focal length, but whatever is in the view is captured. We can't keep stuff out; it's photographic by-catch. One process is additive—what shall we include in this drawing?—the other subtractive—when will those people leave so I can get a shot of the building?

As a child, I made many drawings of my world: the living room of our family house on Jefferson Street, with such detail that I can identify the furniture (see Figure 4.3); the den of my grandparent's house on Avenham Avenue, with the creases and folds of the pillows (see Figure 4.4). I remember being very proud of that, because I knew how important drawing fabric was to the mastery of the craft. It was all about the drapery. Looking at these drawings done by my child-self I remember the places themselves and my youthful obsession with trying to

FIGURE 4.3 My childhood drawing of our living room, including a drawing of a photograph on the wall—a double indicative.

FIGURE 4.4 My grandparents' den, drawn when I was older and fixated on fabric.

draw as well as my mother did. I think I thought that I did draw as well as she did. I remember thinking that I thought I did.

We draw to remember; the act of drawing itself engraves a place into our minds. I'm not talking, however, about a Proustian wallow in remembrances of things drawn, because memory—and the artifacts it provokes and produces— is actually a useful thing. This is particularly true for architects, who draw constantly and for very different reasons than child-I did. Then, I made drawings that function in the present as memory-props; now as an architect I make drawings because, like Zumthor, I want to understand something and I might want to use that understanding at some point in the future. Before we can make the drawings that point toward a possible world—design drawings—we make drawings that capture some aspect of the world. In other words, before we can draw toward the world, we draw from it. That, however, is not entirely or always obvious to architecture students.

Recently I worked with a student with whom I had significant communications issues. We'll call her N—the names, as in the previous chapter, have been changed to protect, well, everybody—and she was beginning her thesis. She admitted to me that she wasn't very familiar with the city...any city, apparently. She seemed perplexed about how to find information about the essential facts of the place—lot lines, floor area ratios, height restrictions, and even the tidal swing of the river. I'm not sure she knew that the Potomac is a tidal river.

Most of our surreally frustrating conversation, though, focused on a drawing of the waterfront of Alexandria (see Figure 4.5) that she had found online and downloaded to use as a base for her site drawing. On her digital copy, however, she had dialed down the original color so it was a bouquet of candy-land pastels. The original drawing, which was either hand-drawn or a careful simulation of hand-drawn, served as the underlay over which she had drafted on a layer of trace the perimeters of the city blocks in black lines. Nothing between the original and the overlay really aligned though, nor were things misaligned in any predictable way, as when a tracing slips and the entire drawing can be righted by moving the paper around. I tried. Had her drawing been a true-measure survey of these blocks of the city, which she then had layered onto a Kevin Lynchian[1] psychometric map of experienced dimensions, I would have been fascinated. One could certainly make a drawing like that, which would record which city blocks felt short when walked, or which were so haptically dull that they seemed to stretch for miles, overlaid onto the true measure of the city's blocks. A drawing like that would be illuminating, and potentially a useful bit of urban design rhetoric, which might lead to other questions that mined the gap between measure and perception. Are there corners that feel sharper? What makes a block feel too long? What makes it just right? Unfortunately, that's not what she was doing.

Her drafted outlines of city blocks met at sharp right angles, overriding the eased radii of the hand-drawn corners visible on the drawing below. That seemed odd to me. Think for a minute about how you might make a drawing of a

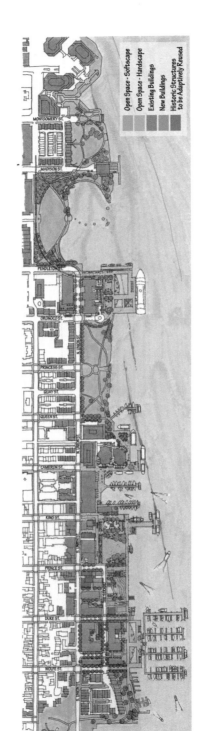

FIGURE 4.5 The Olin Studio's master plan for the Alexandria waterfront is color-coded to help a viewer sort out what is existing and what is proposed.

neighborhood or a district of city blocks: let's say the blocks are about 250' on a side, and the street width between each block is 40' (see Figure 4.6). You might tick off those dimensions first along an east–west line, then along a north–south line, or some other convenient anchor for a typical American 90-degree grid. You would then have a plaid drawing, with major and minor spaces suggestive of possible blocks and streets. If you wanted to make sure that you were drawing a particular set of blocks, you'd have to measure each one, curb to curb, because reality is rarely so exactly repetitive. Some blocks might be 250', a few 230', and maybe a real outlier or two at 267'. Of course we all know, because we are in the world, that curbs do not come to 90-degree corners, mitered like a picture frame. To draw a city block that matches most worlds, you must set your compass—oh, how I date myself—or pick your radius tool, and ease the corners into the quarter circle we all know from walking in the world.

Those who design streets for a living know that the looseness or tightness of that corner radius has a surprisingly profound effect on pedestrian safety and quality of life. So, the next step in that drawing would be to decide exactly what that radius should be for the quarter circle corners. If you're an urban designer of some skill, and you're working on a traffic calming strategy, you might do that by hand on an overlay of trace paper. In that case, the drafted lines on the under-layer would have provided measured anchors to the hand-sketched propositions on the over-layer about the actual shape of the corners. A crisply drafted grid is a great ally, serving the same purposes, as my father used to say, that a lamppost serves the inebriated: for both illumination and support. In this way, a drawing would

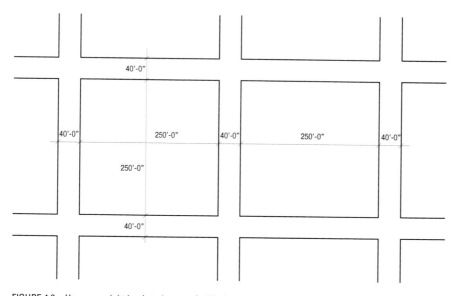

FIGURE 4.6   How one might begin to lay out city blocks.

eventually be produced that would bring the hand-drawn curves into a geometric specificity that could be translated into the real world by somebody with a tape measure. Because it takes more time—it's an additional step in the drawing—to make a radiused corner, you would do that on a layer of trace on top of the drafted rectangle blocks. You need that lamppost. But in N's case, the layers were reversed: the hand-drawn was the under-layer; the drafted layer was the traced one. This is why I was so deeply puzzled by N's drawing(s).

These thoughts ran through my mind—a lot runs through my mind while I'm talking to my students—but instead of sharing it all with her, I just asked, "Where did this under-layer come from? Did you draw it?"

"No."
"Who did?"
"I don't know."
"Why did you choose it?"
"I found it, and I wanted to show the city and the river," she said
"There are many images that show the city and the river," I pressed on. "The City of Alexandria has maps, and of course, there's the old fave, Google," I said. I was trying to be helpful and supportive, shifting my linguistic register from consultative/professorial to casual.
She gave me a blank stare.
"You need to keep track of where you find stuff. It's just basic scholarship," I said. She could tell that I was getting exasperated.
"Ok," she said, and made a note in her sketchbook, probably something to the effect of "Susan likes to know where things come from."

I looked more closely at the original drawing. It was drawn *as if* by hand, and perhaps was by hand. The lines wiggled just so, as if the anonymous drafter or algorithm was over-caffeinated.[2] The lines outlining the buildings crossed a bit at the corners, the east–west lines overrunning the north–south lines, in mannered imitation of an archaic drafting technique. The landscape bits, indistinct tree and shrub-like things, were squiggled suggestively and washed in green. The Potomac River was implausibly blue. Some of what was drawn was existing; some of it proposed. Good luck guessing which was which. The original, as you can see, has a key to inform the viewer what different colors mean, denoting what is existing and what is proposed, but N hadn't retained that information in her copy.

I had to ask her bluntly, "Is this a drawing of the city *as it is* or the city as you *wish it were*?" And, yes, I asked it just like that, in the subjunctive mode. I'm not sure that helped.

She gave me another blank stare and said, "That's my site, and that's the way it is."

I pointed to a block just off Prince Street, near the river. "Is that there? That building?"

"Yes," she nodded, "it is. It has a fence around it."

"Does it have all those little café tables so delightfully sprinkled beside it?" I pointed to the entourage.

"No," she said, "there's a fence around it. And, no, all that stuff isn't there."

So I asked her again, "Is this a drawing of the place *as it is* or *as it might be?*"

We went on and on like this for a while longer. Students who were sitting nearby slithered away one by one, desperate for coffee or determined that now might be a good time to start smoking. I finally suggested that she and I head out the door right now, walk six blocks east, and together see if in fact the world matched this drawing. I knew, of course, that it didn't. It only matched the drawing in certain places, but not at all in others, which, if mindfully crafted, can be an effective strategy to show how new things will fit in with existing things. Otto Eggers, as we saw in the last chapter, was a master of this game of direction of fit. A drawing such as this one, which establishes the ground truth of what exists and what doesn't, must contain denotations to clue the viewer in to which bits are indicative and which are subjunctive. The original drawing did, but N had manipulated it by deploying the delicious filters and color tricks that Photoshop offers, with the result that the essential distinctions in the original—grey represented existing buildings; pink, new; bright pink for existing but reborn—were gone. She had eliminated even from her own eyes the key distinctions among the signifiers of the presently real and the potentially real. She bristled when I suggested that she was using the image decoratively, but an image drained of information and rendered meaningless can only be decorative.

What I was desperately seeking from N, and what she should have been striving for herself, was an unequivocal drawing of the existing conditions, the situation as it is.[3] Such drawings bear the responsibility of fidelity to some aspect of the so-called real world; they pledge allegiance to the truth. It is their responsibility to match the world. When we look at a drawing, we need to know if it depicts something that exists, something that doesn't, perhaps something that can't exist, or if it is an instruction for making something exist. We can be pretty sure, because the historical documentation supports it, that the Baptistery in Florence existed when Brunelleschi drafted it into service for his perspective demonstration. Florentines could look at his drawing, raise their eyes to the building, and say, "Ecco! It does look like that!"—or words to that effect. It is a reaction that is more dramatic but not so different from my own joy in recognizing chairs, pie safes, and pillows that I remember from my childhood *lebensweldt*. It wasn't long, though, before clever architects and painters were using the same technique to represent buildings and rooms that didn't exist, constructing on canvas and plaster entirely fictional buildings occupying fictional space as if real.[4] Artists can represent things that can't exist but it's a fair question whether that's something architects should do intentionally. If the language of the drawing is ambiguous— naïvely so or will-fully deceptive—how are we to know if the subject of a painting or drawing exists somewhere out in the world, off the paper or canvas?

While art historians can enjoy fruitful careers arguing about which real landscapes or buildings are represented in various paintings, the stakes are some-what different for architectural drawings. It really matters. N's manipulated draw-ing of the Alexandria waterfront contained just enough truth to be convincingly misleading. To a viewer without direct experience of the city, the drawing was *as if* true; to one who knows the city, it was a puzzling piece of deception. If a drawing is representing a possible building, then it is a subjunctive drawing, about which too much will be said in the next chapter. If a drawing is representing a "real" building—or site, a city, or a landscape—that currently sits somewhere on this earth or did at some time in the past, then it is an indicative drawing.

Those are really the only two options, as we discussed in the previous chapter, since we have followed James's lead and collapsed the three modes—indicative, subjunctive, imperative—into an effective two; thus the imperative and the subjunctive together face off against the indicative across reality.[5] An indicative drawing is a pointing-out, a description of a factual condition; they are intended to match the world. As in language, an indicative statement can be evaluated accord-ing to its veracity; in other words, factual statements can be true or false. In an indicative drawing, a line has an immediate correspondence to a real condition and therefore the consistency of the narrative is essential. A drawing can't be three-quarters true any more than a verbal description should be. One false or mis-leading line in an indicative drawing is a thirteenth chime of the clock, as the saying goes, undermining the authority of the entire drawing. An indicative drawing must be nothing but the truth, although, because every drawing involves editing and selecting which bits of reality get invited to the image, it can never be the whole truth.

Yet, it would be inaccurate to say that the role of indicative drawings is only to show what things "look like." They may do so, but only as a consequence of showing what things *are*. All indicatives are not the same. As Goodman puts it,

> For a picture to be faithful is simply for the object represented to have the properties that the picture in effect ascribes to it. But such fidelity or correctness or truth is not a sufficient condition for literalism or realism.[6]

It is impossible to represent the entire truth of the world, to make a complete one-to-one description of a thing into a reduction such as a drawing. Goodman goes on to talk about the different requirements for interpretation of these different types of indicative representations.[7] A perspective sketch of a streetscape or plaza (see Figure 4.7), on the other hand, requires a minimum of interpretation, depending

FIGURE 4.7 Little interpretation and no special code are necessary to understand that this represents a street, as seen from above.

on the context and the audience. It falls to the one doing the drawing to determine exactly which aspects of the world he wants to extract for representation. This is an essential, non-negotiable part of the design process, as architects usually don't work directly on the site of their possible projects, Jersey Devil and a few other design/build practices notwithstanding. Rather, they have to hunt and gather, fill their sketchbooks and memory cards with facts and features of the site to haul back to the studio. In this way, the first act of translation is from the real world into the design world.

What information about the world will I need back at my office? Which chunks of information can I gather from direct observation and which ones are latent, concealed from view, such as property lines, utilities, and buildable envelopes? We'll look at a few of the typical indicative drawings in the architect's playbook. Some are tools for analysis, boiling off excess detail to show only a selection of key facts; others are legal descriptions, necessary to determine where one has agency to act; others still are records, so called "as-builts"; and finally, there are the memory drawings, travel sketches, and visual notes. What they all share is an obligation to define the set of facts to match, and then to do so faithfully.

Analytic indicative drawings extract a set of essential facts for representation in what we might call binary drawings. These are drawings that show only two things but, by extension, also show the relationship between them. The figure–ground (see Figure 4.8) is probably the best known binary drawing in architecture, and is among the go-to drawings for initial site analysis. Others can include

FIGURE 4.8   A figure-ground drawing of ten blocks in Alexandria.

shadow studies, land use, public/private space, and pretty much any other set of facts or data set that can be represented graphically.[8] In the case of figure–ground drawings the relevant information is solid stuff and empty space. The rules of a true figure–ground are simple: buildings—everything within and including their bounding walls—are treated as solid objects, the space between them as noth-ingness. There are no lines in a figure–ground, no curbs, no pavement. Concep-tually, a figure–ground is effectively an inkblot, the mark left behind after an inked building steps on the ground. Such a drawing can only tell you very specific things, like a heartbeat through a stethoscope. And as the heartbeat is to the internist the figure–ground is to an urbanist: a diagnostic tool that telegraphs age, health, and circulation. Consider the fragment of Alexandria represented in the figure–ground in Figure 4.8. What does it tell us? If we know what to look for we can surmise the age of the place, the mobility technologies present at its birth, and make educated guesses about ownership and function. What information does it withhold? Every-thing else. Still, other ichnographic[9] drawings, cousins of the figure–ground, can map additional information onto building footprints or lots, such as relative age, zoning, or land values (see Figure 4.9).

What makes a figure–ground drawing so useful is that either the sol-ids or voids can play the part of the figure or the ground. Figural space shaped and bounded by buildings indicates a certain breed of urban space, traditional and hierarchical; figural buildings, on the other hand, indicate modern space,

Older <——> Younger

FIGURE 4.9 This modified figure-ground telegraphs information about the relative ages of buildings, thanks to the key provided.

undifferentiated and limitless. Figure–grounds are useful mostly at a scale larger than a single building or neighborhood, one large enough to see patterns, where there is sufficient ground for figures to emerge, as in this snippet of the City of Alexandria. And, although a figure–ground purports to be simply a binary drawing of building and space, solid and void, it always bears the full weight of the cultural meanings of "traditional," "hierarchical," "modern," and "undifferentiated." Even though these drawings seem so reductive, as if they were the first act of creation separating the solids from the voids, a simple indicative figure–ground cannot escape the burden of bias and cultural context.

The lack of a clear representation of the facts of her site was what drained my patience with N. Facts can't be tossed in a salad with opinions and possibilities. It's indigestible. Whether a site is in fact empty or not can be determined by direct observation, but not all the relevant facts of a site are visible. That said, in a compact city one can often deduce property lines, set-backs, and height limits by looking at the consistency of a street wall or cornice line. These built epiphenomena are good indicators that there are, or were, a set of rules about how much could be built where. But the kickable world isn't always so reliable. Plat plans, a crucial type of drawing that reveals the hidden lines of ownership and utilities, have the force of legal documents (see Figure 4.10). The information represented in plats serves to illustrate and reinforce a verbal description. Survey drawings have their own language, combining words, numbers, and graphics, and this "curious mixture" of information, to invoke Goodman again, must be internally consistent.

Drawings of this kind are allergic to any graphic ornamentation. The information can't tolerate proximity to, or intrusions of, subjectivity and so they are the least likely drawing type to be experienced aesthetically. A plat requests just the facts. For some of us—I admit it—there is a real pleasure in looking at a figure–ground. If it documents a city I know and love I can augment my affection for places—the Piazza Navona in Rome looks great in figure–ground—with the satisfaction of finding patterns and correlations, such as a chain of piazzas linked, or the continuity of an axis. Very few of us, probably including surveyors, gaze at plat plans in the same reverie. All indicative drawings have a high truth-to-beauty ratio and the farther they are on the scale toward legal documents—the more they denote rather than depict—the less they are conflated with art. They may even become suspect if they are too appealing, provoking suspicions akin to those surrounding too-beautiful rhetoric. The next two indicative types we'll discuss, however, coalesce truth and beauty in the craft of making the drawing itself.

Remember the anecdote from the last chapter in which Francis James describes the difference between the two kinds of drawings an architect might have: one is his "blueprint," the other his "record:" "Now consider an artist's sketch of the house after it is built. He intends for the sketch, which is his 'record,' to match the world."[10] James's knowledge of architecture and the design process may be equal to my knowledge of functional linguistics, but that doesn't stop

FIGURE 4.10   A cropped plat of adjacent properties.

either of us from charging on, using each other's disciplines as illuminating met-
aphors for our own. (Despite popular usage of the term, no one in the design
professions calls such drawings "blueprints.") It's more accurate to say that one
drawing is his design, or subjunctive, drawing; the other, his as-built, or indicative,
drawing. James hypothesizes that the two drawings might appear identical, which
is essential to his point that there must be tell-tale signs, marks, or media to clue a
viewer to each drawing's direction of fit. Which way is the from/to arrow pointing?
For an as-built, the arrow points directly from the world to the drawing.

The drawing standards of the Historic American Building Survey (HABS),
and its close cousins, the Historic American Engineering Record (HAER) and
Historical American Landscape Survey (HALS), are among the best examples of
this factual clarity: these drawings express *conditions coincident with fact.* They
are truthful drawings; they match the world in specific ways. HABS drawings are
charged with "documenting the historic buildings, sites, structures, and objects
of this country by producing measured drawings, large format photographs, and
written histories."[11] Standard II states that such documentation "shall be prepared accurately from reliable sources with limitations clearly stated to permit

independent verification of information" and further, that "no part of the measured drawings shall be produced from hypothesis or non-measurement-related activities.[12] The independent verification and the caveat against conjecture are essential; these documentations must be accurate in their depictions/descriptions of their subjects. Those making the drawings cannot just willfully add stuff they think should be there or might have been there.

Look closely at these drawings (see Figures 4.11, 4.12, and 4.13) for the Lockkeeper's House, an early nineteenth-century building at 17th Street and Constitution Avenue in Washington, D.C. A visit to that corner today will leave one puzzled about exactly what lock was being kept, but when it was built in 1832, the little building sat at the edge of a canal that ran from the Potomac across the National Mall. Our brief experiment with Venetian mobility technologies was killed by the railroad, and so now this lonely little building sits a couple of miles from its mother river, a curious reminder of a past possible future. It requires no special skill or professional insight to determine that the drawing in Figure 4.13 depicts the building in the photograph (see Figure 4.14). It passes the accuracy test, but not at all scales and not everywhere. Look at how the stone is drawn, and look at how the stone *is*. This is a hand drawing, not a digital one, done in 1994. Some lines are drafted, assisted by the straightedges of parallel bars and triangles; others are done freehand, such as the incomplete stone coursing, which just fades out around the door as if that were as far as the drafter could reach. And, if you look really carefully, you'll see that the stones that are drawn don't exactly match the real ones; they're accurate in an "it goes something like this" way, but not in the same way that archaeological drawings are, where the shape and location of each stone or post-hole is a matter of scientific evidence.[13] These instances of graphic ellipses are not willful deceptions; they are informationally sufficient, frugal even, and no more detailed than necessary.

Together the photograph in Figure 4.14 and the drawing in Figure 4.13, with its textual and numerical notations, serve to corroborate one another; the drawings and photograph match each other and the world. The drawn line, plus a few key words naming an object or a material, plus a numerical dimension string or two, creates a set of mutually reinforcing information, so long as none of it is contradictory. Each bit of information increases the tightness of the match to the world. Likewise the relative sizes, the scale, of things shouldn't contradict the drawing; we expect that a dimension drawn in one place will plausibly be the same in another. If several drawings at different scales inhabit the same sheet, as in the informationally heterogeneous Site Plan in Figure 4.11, then each one needs its own measure.

The indicative drawings we do in the field or while travelling come in the same flavors as other architectural drawings—plans, sections, elevations, perspectives, and various forms of diagramming. Some aim at depiction and the best are beautiful and evocative, triggering memories of iconic places for the one

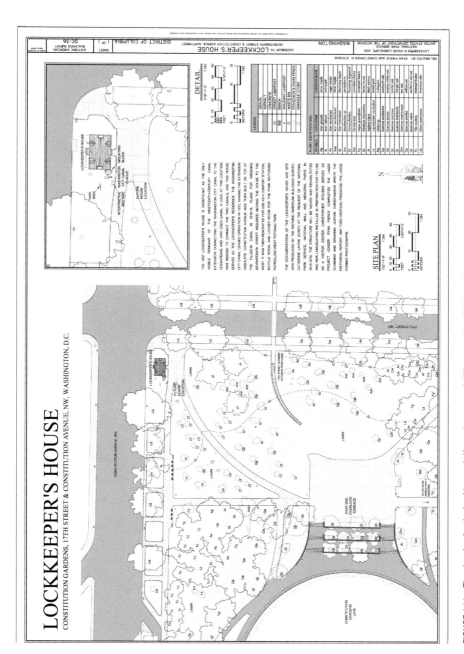

FIGURE 4.11 The site plan for the Lockkeeper's House has several different scales of information. This set of drawings was executed by a team of faculty and students from California Polytechnic State University in 1994 for the Historic American Building Survey.

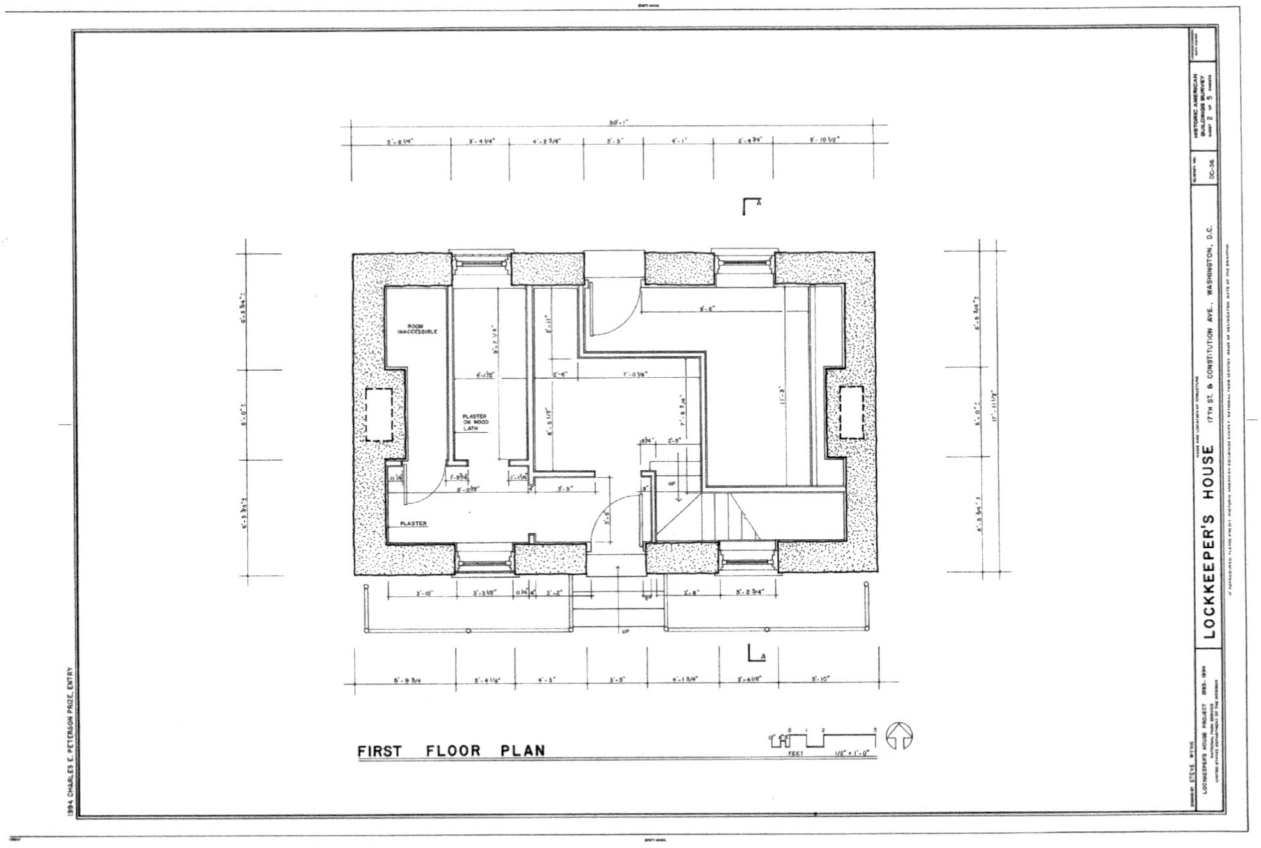

FIGURE 4.12 The Lockkeeper's plan.

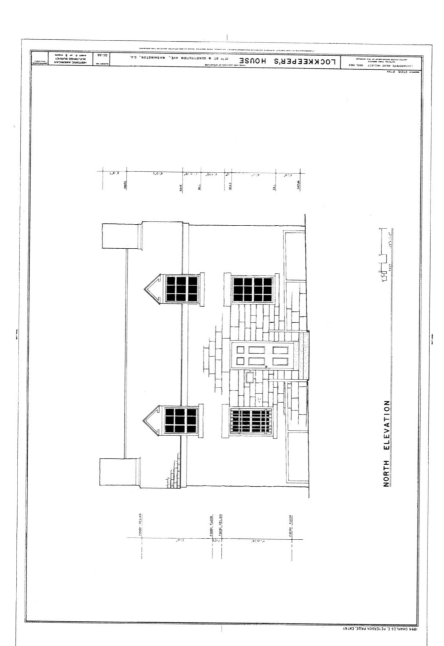

FIGURE 4.13 The Lockkeeper's elevation, with the suggestion of continuous stone.

FIGURE 4.14 A photograph of the Lockkeeper's House taken in 1934, by Albert S. Burns, part of the documentation of the building for the Historic American Building Survey.

who made the sketch and anyone else who recognizes the place. They are as abstracted—literally, "drawn from"—from the real world as the analytic drawings, and for the same reasons: if you are trying to grab every shred of the world in front of your eyes you would be better off taking a photograph. Sketching from the world inevitably leaves a lot of the world behind. That's why we can think of these drawings as mnemonics. A mnemonic isn't the memory itself in full; it's the distillation, the synecdoche, that can reanimate the whole.

Consider these two cityscape sketches, one from Siena (see Figure 4.15) and one from Zurich (see Figure 4.16). They are my own sketches, and so my own memories too. Without the little notes at the bottom of each, I'm not sure I would have remembered exactly when and where they were drawn, but encyclopedic memory isn't the value here. These two drawings remind me that once there were moments when I sat sufficiently still, and attended sufficiently to the world, to draw something essential from what I saw. In Siena, it is the city as a pile of blocks, not easily separated from one another, with no clear volumes of air

FIGURE 4.15   An indicative drawing of the rooftops of Siena.

FIGURE 4.16   An indicative "café view" of a street in Zurich.

between things. In this Cézanne-ish assembly, a few details of charming banality stand out: quite a few television antennae, shutters, and an awning. In Zurich—captioned "café view, last night"—the focus of my attention was the carved slice of sky made by the edges of cornices and roofs. As in Siena, there are bits of balcony, shutters, and a pair of barely-there flags. I know that the sky was what interested me because I can see in the drawing that I heavied up the profile line of where the buildings meet the sky. Through the drawing, I can read my own thoughts at a distance of years.

What do these drawings continue to say to me as an urbanist now? I'm not going to design a self-consciously picturesque hill town, so how do these drawings work? They are, channeling Peter Zumthor, "reservoirs of the architectural atmospheres and images"[14] that I value: compact urbanity, expressions of individual life, a public realm from which one can sit, gaze, and sketch. In that way, I am *in* the sketch because it represents my point of view; the fact it is on paper at all, in graphite, says, "this place is important for the reasons depicted here." Here, in such drawings, viewers get to travel, to inhabit my place and see what I saw.

There is a difference between indicative drawings that say, "I want to remember this" and those that say, "I want to *understand* this." One could make the argument that a photograph is a far more efficient way to satisfy the desire to remember, but a photograph is rarely capable of dissecting reality so the viewer can understand it. In the previous chapter, we talked about *parti* and bubble diagrams as among the early drawings that an architect might do to translate different types of client prompts into graphic form. Those diagrams can also be deployed indicatively to reveal relationships that require some effort to see.

On the same trip where I drew Siena and Zurich,[15] we visited the Villa Gamberaia outside of Florence. I had not looked at the plan of the garden before we went, although I'm sure we told the students to do so; therefore I spent much of my time there trying to understand the formal structure of the place. In fact, I helpfully titled my sketch (see Figure 4.17) "diagram of axes & enclosure elements @ Villa Gamberaia" as an additional memory nudge. The different marks and media I used provide clues to my process of understanding through drawing. The building is recognizable where the black pen line traces the enclosing walls

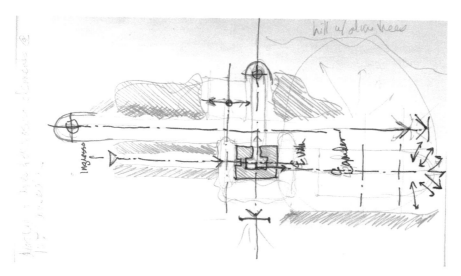

FIGURE 4.17   My sketch of the Gamberaia garden, as I tried to understand it.

with certainty; the grey hatching within confesses that I'm not considering the interior in relation to the garden. There are "center lines" drawn according to the architecture convention, a concise grapheme/morpheme mash-up, with the "C" hooked onto the dash-dot line, which in turn does double-duty as the vertical line of the "L." Deployed here, these lines demark various axes and cross-axes. There are grey hatched blobs that represent topiary and thick planting, green *poché*.[16] There are a few words—"*ingresso*," "hill with olive trees"—to describe things easier said than drawn. Finally, along with the two unaligned centerlines of the villa and the garden, there are a few arrows to remind one to look this way or walk that way. Ink and graphite, words and marks, lines and shading, combine to make this little field sketch a dense indicative. When I finally looked at an actual drawing of the Gamberaia Garden (see Figure 4.18) I was pleasantly surprised at how accurate my reading of the situation had been, although I missed the slight trapezoidal shape of the section across from the house. I remain puzzled by the two center-lines, but it's also clear from my garden elevation drawing (see Figure 4.19) that the house was then, and remains, indifferent to them.

Other field drawings represent attempts to understand the construction of things. These sketches of details, connections, and moments occupy the opposite end of the indicative scale from diagrams, drawing closely from the physical, even if both aim to uncover how physical or spatial elements are related to one another. This sketch (see Figure 4.20) was drawn at the Sackler Galleries of the Royal Academy in London and, as the caption claims, it focuses on the relationship between the old and new parts of the building. There are many—although not unlimited—architectural ways for old and new to relate to one another; in this case, they relate across a synapse, in a kind of unconsummated kiss, declining to engage physically. There are very real practical and structural reasons why the new might chose to leave the old alone—uncertainty over what loads or stresses the old could bear, preservationist concerns over irreparable damage to the body—but there are also architectural/aesthetic reasons. Michelangelo could have painted God and Adam shaking hands, which would have had quite a bro vibe, but he didn't. Instead, there is no more figural gap in the history of art, a moment of emptiness so charged with anticipation that it is the very subject of the painting.[17]

So it is in this little architectural moment: the longing between new and old is undone by the impossibility of its fulfillment. I was, as you can tell, enthralled by this moment, and tried to draw not so much what it looked like as what it *was*: a cantilevered glass floor supported on steel tubes, unapologetically invading the frieze space of the old cornice, itself a *poché* cantilever. This moment is in the light well, a crack between the original building and a later nineteenth-century addition and, as in the fractal principle of self-similarity, it is a crack—or more architecturally, a reveal—at all scales, from the building to this detail. It is the kind of detail, as Marco Frascari famously said, that tells the tale.[18]

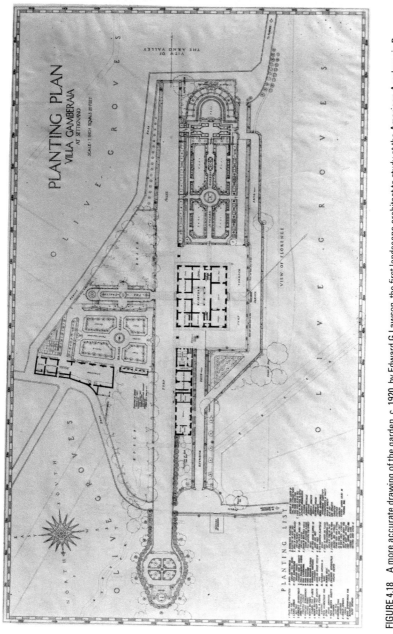

FIGURE 4.18   A more accurate drawing of the garden, c. 1920, by Edward G Lawson, the first landscape architect to study at the American Academy in Rome.

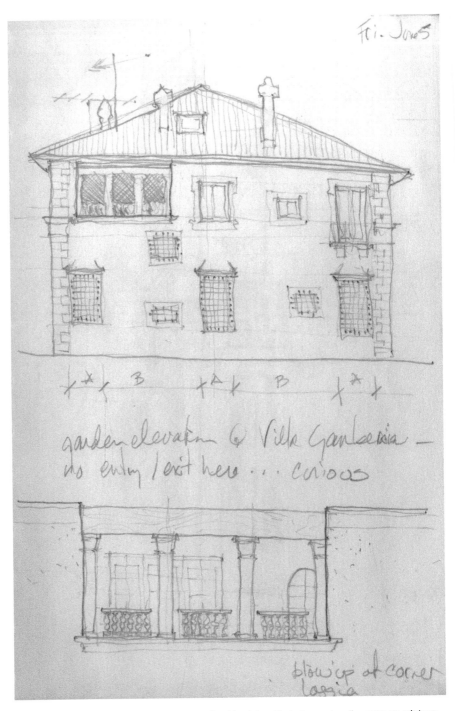

FIGURE 4.19 I remained puzzled about the relationship of the villa to the garden: "no entry or exit here... curious."

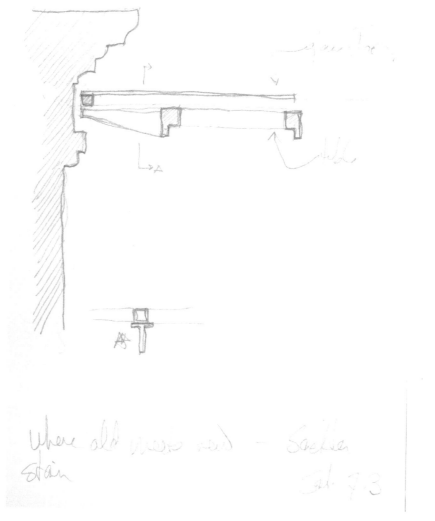

FIGURE 4.20   Old and new are getting quite close to one another in Foster + Partners' 1991 addition to the Sackler Galleries in London.

Before we can design, there is always an existing condition to document—in drawings, photographs, notes, and numbers—and one isn't free to pick and choose which parts of reality to match. You can, and must, leave some information out; it is both a tired trope and an irrefutable truth that something is lost in translation. You can tease the real bits apart into different layers or drawings, but you can't just mix your wishes into the same matter as reality without thoughtful consideration of a clear representational strategy. An indicative drawing can host subjunctive representations but the author of such drawings needs to stay on the correct side of the line between deception and documentation. Furthermore, as we will discuss in the next chapter, a subjunctive drawing can welcome indicative information; in fact, effective depictions of wishes often depend on indicative allies to strengthen their rhetorical power.

All drawings, including the full spectrum of indicative drawings, are abstractions as well as constructions. That word derives from Latin, as so many of these delicious words do, and it means, literally, "to draw away from" (*ab +* *trahere*). Indicative drawings draw from the world but, as I hope is clear from this chapter, it is not a mechanical or rote process. Abstraction is a creative act of selection and representation. Goodman says it best: "In sum, effective representation and description require invention. They are creative. They inform each other; and they form, relate, and distinguish objects."[19] The first act of translation from building to drawing sets the table where the architect begins the acts of transformation, which define the design process and precede the translation back from drawing to building.[20] The fruitfulness of the entire process depends on the fullness of the indicative representation, and at their best, these drawings literally re-present the world to us, readying the known yet unexamined world for design action.

NOTES

1. See Kevin Lynch's classic study of how people perceive their environments, *The Image of the City*.
2. Why would I doubt the existence of a human author for this drawing? Because digital technologies are challenging the credibility of drawings on multiple levels.
3. Later that semester N changed her project and her site. She also decided to remove me from her thesis committee. Sometimes, it is just not a good match.
4. For more on this, see Edward Robbins, who covers this dilemma and its consequences for architecture as a social practice in his book *Why Architects Draw*.
5. James collapses the three modes to demonstrate that the subjunctive no longer exists as a formal structure in English. He suggests there are two modes in English: the imperative and the indicative. For our purposes, which are not linguistic, I would suggest that the imperative is a subset of the subjunctive, not the other way round,

6. Goodman, *Languages of Art*, P 36.
7. Ibid.
8. The field of data visualization or infographics could be its own category here as these images can create entirely new representations of places. See my earlier book with the National Building Museum, *Intelligent Cities*, in particular Laura Kurgan's essay on her "Million Dollar Block" visualizations on page 45.
9. A delicious word with a simple meaning—essentially a plan of building(s).
10. WJames, *Semantics of the English Subjunctive*, P 12.
11. *HABS/HAER Standards*, front matter. Again, a heterogeneous mix of denotations, descriptions, and depictions.
12. Ibid, P 6.
13. I have to put on my Luddite shoes at this point and argue that only the human eyes and hand can make such a drawing from life. We can now, however, extract that information digitally from a photograph.
14. Zumthor, *Thinking Architecture* P 10
15. Part of this trip was a study-abroad with students. I produced a copious amount of sketches to try to model the behavior I expected from them. I wish I could say that such graphic productivity is typical for me, but words tend to outnumber drawings in my little black books. Surprise.
16. Another great French architectural word, like *parti*, *poché* is the mystery stuff inside a solid, and is deployed graphically when the insides aren't the important part of the drawing or when we don't really know what's in there..
17. You know the one. If not, see Michelangelo's *Creation of Adam*, Sistine Chapel, 1510-ish.
18. Marco Frascari's influential essay, "The Tell-the-Tale Detail," first published in 1981 and widely available in PDF form online, proposes that far from being a set of technical problems to be worked out by others lower down the design hierarchy, architectural/construction details can be understood as primary generators of a building's form.
19. Goodman, *Languages of Art*, P 33.
20. I owe the late J. Thomas Regan credit for that succinct and elegant way of describing the design process.

CHAPTER 5
WISHES AND INSTRUCTIONS

If wishes were horses, beggars would ride.

Old English proverb

All buildings begin as someone's wish. At the groundbreaking for the construction of the East Building of the National Gallery in Washington, D.C., architect I. M. Pei introduced his wife to Bill Mann, the project manager for Charles Tompkins and Co., the contractor, saying "This is the man who will make my dreams come true."[1] We usually think of making dreams come true as the stuff of Disney films or fairy tales, but it is really the stuff of architecture. We also don't usually think of a contractor—picture the clichéd burly, hard hat-wearing, pragmatic foil to the Armani suit-wearing, visionary architect—as the one who is in the business of making dreams come true, but that is how Pei introduced him, probably with his characteristic luminous smile. Mann, in fact, became the final custodian of the East Building dream, a dream that began in the mind of J. Carter Brown, then the director of the National Gallery. It was then implanted, Filarete-style, into the mind of Pei, shared iteratively through the language of drawings among his staff, and with Brown and his board, until it became a fully formed wish, and then a set of instructions, for a new building.

The idea for the National Gallery expansion dates to the 1960s, when the soon-to-be director J. Carter Brown was still an assistant.[2] Needled by a colleague for working in a museum with a stellar collection but no place dedicated to scholarship, Brown drafted a document outlining a proposal for what would become CASVA, the Center for the Advanced Studies in the Visual Arts.[3] Brown was put in charge of this ambitious project: "Then at a certain point, the trustees said, there's going to be a new building, I should really be assigned to that project...the first step would be to choose an architect."[4] It was an auspicious choice; Brown was a self-described "architecture buff" and confessed that he had wanted to be an architect—second choice to firefighter—when he grew up. Instead, he grew up to be a significant client, whose verbal and visual ambitions and wishes were essential to the design and construction of the new wing of the National Gallery.

In that respect, Director Brown is little different from our space-challenged homeowner in Chapter 3 but instead of her stack of shelter publications he has images in his mind of other buildings. As preparation for the project, he and Pei had toured the museums of Europe for a month. Brown had some ideas of his own. He knew that the odd shape of the site—a troublesome trapezoid at the confluence of three major streets—would be a challenge and he made clear that he wasn't interested in an axial, neo-classical solution. Yet, in the very early stage of East Building dreaming, it's clear that his mind was open to possibilities: "I was very impressed by Moshe Safdie's Habitat in the Montreal World's Fair. I thought it might be delicious to have that site, since it has a wacky shape anyway, be broken up into a kind of Greek village of small boxes."[5] Delicious perhaps but, in hindsight, extremely difficult to imagine. To our eyes now, Pei's iconic pink marble prism presents itself as the obvious, irrefutable solution. How could it be otherwise? That's the curious thing about buildings: when the wish becomes a reality all the other possible wishes evaporate and it becomes difficult even to imagine that anyone had entertained any other notions.

The essence of the design process—that mysterious period that begins when the client conveys her aspirations to the architect and ends with a building that inevitably is at once the answer to and yet more and other than the original request—is this gradual shift in language from the articulation of a wish to a set of instructions, as the architect seeks to get the recalcitrant world to match his ideas. The entire journey is a subjunctive one. Although it may seem at first that we end with imperatives—"do this" instead of "if we were to do this"— the illocutionary force is more subtle than that. At this point we have to enlist more species of the subjunctive mode to make finer distinctions among these wishful drawings, because some are imaginative representations and some are deontic representations, that is, representations directed toward an action. This term, "deontic," which we introduced previously, refers to a duty or obligation and therefore a "deontic expression" is more than a mere speculation or a wish. It carries the implication of action to follow, as with drawings that are instructions for making buildings. According to Lynn Berk, the deontic mode contains a variety of directives, such as orders, strong obligations, suggestions, contractual obligations, reprimands, permissions, and requests.[6] The two types of subjunctive that are most relevant here are the "volitional," sometimes called the "optative," and the "jussive," sometimes called the "mandative." Volitional expressions, i.e. design drawings, are expressions of desires, or as Berk puts it, of "wanting, willingness, intention and wishing."[7] Jussive expressions such as construction documents and specifications are instructions for an action the conditions of satisfaction of which they themselves contain. In other, less cumbersome words, referring to their own information, both drawn and written, construction documents say "make it so."

Wishes always precede instructions; you have to know what you want before you figure out how to make it real. Architecture students learn in professional practice class that there are certain fundamental phases of design and that, for budget purposes, these phases should have certain percentages of hours assigned to them.[8] These phases are formalized in the American Institute of Architects' (AIA) Document B101, the "Standard Form of Agreement Between Owner and Architect," and have remained remarkably constant even in the face of significant—and mostly technology-induced—realignments and redefinitions in the design and construction industries, even in the definition of "drawing" itself. Like the five acts of a Shakespearean drama, the Standard Form lists five "basic" services: the schematic design phase, the design development phase, the construction documents phase, the bidding/negotiation phase, and the construction phase.[9] And, as in Shakespeare's plays, the groundwork is laid in the first two phases, when the tensions and motivations of the characters are revealed. The action builds to the climax in the third act, er, phase. Complex story lines of the design—such as facing the reality of budget—are untangled and resolved in the fourth. Finally, the construction phase brings the denouement of the architect's drama when the translation from drawing to building, as Robin Evans puts it, commences. It is tempting to say that at this point the construction drawings are "complete," but in truth this just marks the beginning of a series of antiphonal drawings, which constitute the call and response of change orders and requests for information. This five-act structure traces the arc of the design narrative—the drama of the documents as it were—and cues up the beginning of the sequel, the construction narrative, which has its own drama.

To propel the drama—and push my metaphor to exhaustion—these documents need characters, and something has to happen in each act in order to set up the action in the next. Because it was drafted[10] by attorneys, the Standard Agreement uses different verbs in each phase to describe what the architect is doing: in the first three phases, the architect "prepares" drawings and documents; in the fourth phase, the architect "helps" do a variety of things. In the final phase—construction—the architect "administers" the contract, which, as any administrator knows, harbors its own rodent's nest of other verbs, including but not limited to visiting, reviewing, interpreting, evaluating, arguing, shouting, and cursing. We will focus in this chapter on the "preparing" part of the first three phases, primarily because that's where the drama is, that's where the wishing begins, and that's where the wishes are transformed into instructions.

When I graduated from architecture school my first jobs were at a series of small firms, each for very brief periods of time thanks to a combination of my level of usefulness (low) and the macro-economic situation (lousy and recession-y). Consequently, most of the projects I worked on remained as fictional as my student work. My bosses would assign me a task to add some vegetation to an illustrative site plan, ink some plans with clever grid shifts and grace-note curves, or give an elevation or two a color-pencil facelift, and then it was pencils down because the project would inevitably be put on hold for one reason or another. Then I would be laid off. When I finally spent more than a year at a firm, I was able to see a few little projects through the entire five-act drama. Then I was laid off again and went to work for a corporate firm where the projects were large and complex. They took so long to execute that, with the exception of a now-demolished health club interior, I never again experienced the full five acts. Among the many things about practice that perplexed me in my short, bumpy time there, was the mysterious line between the first and the second acts, between schematic design and design development. As I worked toward a professional understanding of the process, I tried to discern what combination of lines, numbers, and text distinguished these two phases. What exactly did design development need to say that schematic design didn't?

The AIA's Standard Agreement states that during the schematic design phase the architect does a lot of preliminary stuff—looking over the program, the site, the schedule, and the budget—and then "prepares a site plan and preliminary building plans, elevations, and sections; makes preliminary selections of materials and systems." The architect might prepare some other documents, such as "study models, perspective sketches, and digital modeling."[11] If everyone—client, design team, and any regulatory agency involved—is happy with the work, the architect can shake off the adjective "preliminary" and begin Act 2: the preparation of "design development documents that fix and describe the character of the project in plans, elevations, sections, typical construction details, diagrammatic layouts of building systems, outline specifications for materials and systems."[12] Because the drawings are becoming more specific—they are literally drawing nearer to the world—this is also the time to revisit the budget. The shift from schematic design to design development is one of degree, getting closer to this hypothetical thing we're calling "the building," fixing and describing its character. Even the structure of the phrases is different: "design" is a noun in the first phase, the subject modified by the adjective "schematic," but is itself a modifier in the second, where "development" has become the subject. Schematic *design* yields to *design* development. For the most part, these first two phases comprise a conversation between architect and client regarding a shared wish, carried out in a heterogeneous mix of words, images, interpretive sketches, and more, as the architect gives form to—and also augments—the client's wishes.

As we have learned, the subjunctive is the mode to express wishes—whether verbal or graphic—so, while the intensity and the clarity of the language is increasing as we move farther into the design process, it is still in the volitional mode. The drawings are still a wish for something that may be realized or may not, but that can be fully expressed and represented *as if* real. The wishes gradually become hardened and sharpened in the shift from schematic to development. These volitional drawings begin to crawl along a spectrum spanning from generosity to specificity, from productive ambiguity where misreadings and unexpected interpretations can set a design on a different course, to a channelized chute of certainty. The generosity/specificity spectrum takes us from the "as if" to the real. Talking about the information embodied in drawings, Nelson Goodman (from whom I filched the generosity/specificity terminology) says, "[W]e can be as specific or as general as we like about what is exemplified, but we cannot achieve maximum specificity and maximum generosity at the same time."[13] There is a long taper from maximum generosity to maximum specificity in the process from intentionally ambiguous sketches—inchoate wishes—to contract documents. Somewhere in the middle, in the design development phase, is the point of extreme danger where generosity and specificity are roughly equal (see Figure 5.1).

The architect's challenge is to determine when a situation calls for specificity or generosity. A concept approval meeting with the client probably demands more generosity, even productive ambiguity; premature specificity—when a drawing is more accurate than the thinking behind it—will only get you in deep trouble, as my digital-dependent students know all too well. In the opening act of a Shakespearean drama, many things are still possible—the doomed lovers don't yet know they are doomed; the king's rivals could still come to an agreement—but each decision, each misunderstanding, narrows the possibilities for the future. Circumstances and actions throttle the generosity of the early scenes, leading to specific outcomes. It's just like that in the design process, minus—usually—the capital crimes.

A powerful volitional drawing can change the world, even becoming as famous as the final building itself—Maya's Lin's competition entry for the Vietnam Veterans Memorial, Frank Gehry's first squiggle for Bilbao, Bjarke Ingels's cartoon chronicling the birth of the "courtscraper" at West 57th. The origin myth of the

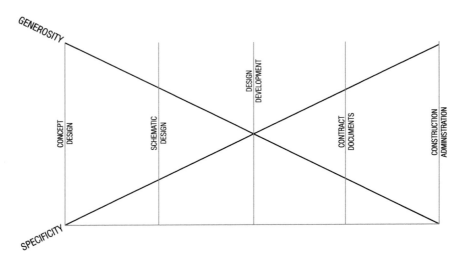

FIGURE 5.1   The different trajectories of generosity and specificity.

East Building of the National Gallery holds that I. M Pei first sketched the *parti* on an envelope, in a stroke of genius apprehending the essential geometry that would drive the building. Pei, however, admits that he doesn't know what happened to that mythic original drawing.[14] Instead, the earliest volitional drawing of the East Building that we do have is this quick sketch in red pen (see Figure 5.2) from Yann Weymouth, Pei's design architect for the building, with the excited handwritten notation at the bottom "IMP sketch first parti! N.G.A. fall 1968".[15] This little drawing—it measures just under eight inches—presents the trapezoidal shape of the site and the right triangles that define the building in red pencil. Pei described the site for the proposed building as "a very difficult one...we couldn't—I could not—ignore the fact that there was a very strong east, west axis coming from Pope's building. The design came that way—how to recognize that axis, accommodate it, and then turn it."[16] That is one of the paradoxes of design: Pei tells us that it was a difficult site, yet his sketch seems effortless. There are no visible erasures or scratching out of lines, only the confident division of the trapezoid into three triangles with the irrefutable axis from John Russell Pope's building drawn as a line with an arrow pointing at the new building. Knowing the building now as a completed work we can't help but see its final form as inevitable, as if emphasized by one of Pei's own red arrows pointing from this first wish straight to the building.

Grey graphite outlines the eastern edge of Pope's National Gallery building—now called the "West Building" to Pei's "East Building"—and indicates a circle in the space between the two. Although Pei has sketched the trapezoidal site—the outer red lines roughly trace the curbs of the bounding streets—it is

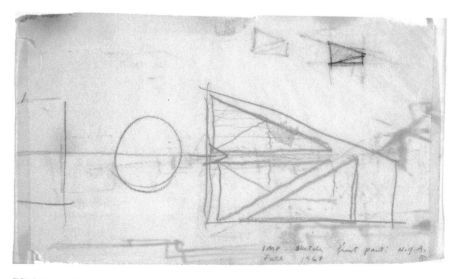

FIGURE 5.2   I. M. Pei's iconic *parti* sketch for the East Building of the National Gallery, 1968.

difficult to read it that way. The outer red line could be the suggestion of the building envelope; the inner triangles would then read as spatial elements, chunks of program, within. The difficulty arises because nowhere else in the drawing does Pei sketch any site information; the crucial diagonal line of Pennsylvania Avenue, which makes the site the trapezoid it is, belongs only to the boundary of the proposed building, not to the larger context of the monumental city. There is very little indicative information in this sketch; very little of the real world has crossed over into the drawn world. Thus the graphite circle floats unmoored in a space that we know is 4th Street. How should we read that circle? If we put ourselves back in 1968, and forget how the building is now, we can read the circle in several ways: as a notation of significance, the way one might circle a word in a paragraph; or as a sign of unifying, of joining; or as an actual formal proposal to make a circular space of some kind. It is also, to use another linguistic analogy, a conjunction, a clear "and" that, along with the red arrow, unites the new building with the old.

Pragmatically, there had to be a physical connection between the two buildings, as they would jointly house the same institution. With what was called the "connecting link" Pei did claim 4th Street, above and below, and as the design drawings for the building show, his circle rolled around quite a bit trying to find a place to be useful. The brief wish-life of the 4th Street circle appears in a series of studies that move from a searching ambiguity in a variety of media to hard-lined near certainty of ink on Mylar, the pre-digital medium of certainty. This drawing, See Figure 5.3, one of the studies of the connecting link, is a reproducible sepia, indicating that some of the information originated on another drawing somewhere else. It shows a lightly drawn single-line outline of the lower level of the East Building. It is sort of a "Nolli" plan,[17] outlining the public space and the auditorium, but leaving out information on anything else. On the west of the drawing is a similar single light line tracing the eastern portion of the existing West Building. Applied to the sepia is a layer of yellow Pantone film,[18] blocking in the area of the connection link, including the future moving walkway and the cafeteria area. The yellow film stretches into the West Building, where new vertical circulation will be located, in an area referred to in the interviews as "project breakthrough." In this drawing, a circle has been cut out of the Pantone and another linear cut parallels the moving walkways. Drawn beneath this plan fragment is a drafted partial section in graphite showing that the circle, so abstract and graphic as a void in the Pantone, was actually envisioned as an oculus open to the sky, perhaps as an homage to Pope's rotunda with its dome and skylit oculus.

The drawing shows the labor involved in its making, three layers of construction and four different media, yet there are no notes, no date, no commentary to reveal what exactly was being studied or who the audience was. Its silence and graphic economy suggest it was an internal study, drawn in the casual register by and for people who already knew the design questions in play at the time. Because it is a reproducible sepia, we know it is the descendant of an original somewhere,

FIGURE 5.3   Pei & Partners' undated study of the "connecting link" from the proposed East Building to the existing West Building.

but also that it had the capacity to be the ancestor of other drawings. There is the implication of its life extending past this particular existence. Before digital technologies made copying and saving files so easy, architects had to choose media that would allow for the continuity of information with minimal loss. Reproducible sepias and "wash-offs"—essentially photocopies on Mylar—provided a base layer of certainty to receive another layer of possibilities. There is so little contrast between the soft and granular lines and the smoky sepia background that the original was probably a pencil drawing on vellum or trace paper. For example, the edge of the existing building must be drawn indicatively and match the world; reality isn't open for manipulation. It belongs to the sepia layer so it will appear automatically and accurately on every subsequent reproduction. It's a waste of effort, and invites signal degradation, to redraw the facts. Reproducible media let the facts persist while the wishes come and go in overdrawings of graphite and Pantone. This obvious sorting of certainty from tentativity has become much more difficult in digital drawing, where every line speaks with the same force, a dilemma about which more will be said in the next chapter.

The circle hangs around for a while, maturing into quasi-certainty, in several plastic-lead-on-Mylar developmental drawings that show the circle rolling around from centered on the axis of the tunnel to finding a home deeper in the cafeteria space and even rolling toward the edges of the space. It tries on possible functions to see which ones are happiest in circular form, from being an open well with a pool at the bottom, to being a raised seating island in the café (see Figure 5.4). Another drawing (there are many, many more; too many to reproduce here) shows that the center has migrated to the outer wall, so that it has become a half-circle labeled "sidewalk café," even though there is no sidewalk.[19] Gone is the giant oculus to the sky, the un-dome. This entire series of studies is marked by erasure scars, combinations of reproducible and reproduced media, and applied Pantone. Translucent sepia is technically erasable, but it leaves such a scar that it always bares the area that was being studied; that part of the drawing is forever marked as "not ready yet." The agony of design can never be erased, even if it now can be deleted.[20]

The drawings produced to study the circle at the connection share certain locutionary characteristics: they all seem to be part of an internal conversation within the architect's office. None of them has the polish, the composition, or the explanatory and supplemental annotations that a presentation drawing would need in order to speak to an extra-professional audience. They are drawings by and for architects, in a context where little or no explanation is necessary because the team brings to the drawing all the understanding required. They are in a graphic shorthand, analogous to what we described earlier as the casual register or tenor, which is efficient for insider conversations but can make interpretation by outsiders difficult. As with conversations among friends, where silences, gestures, and facial expressions bear as much or more meaning than words, this series of unannotated drawings still holds after all these years a productive ambiguity, teetering on the edge of commitment. They are at the wide end of the generosity-to-specificity spectrum when many things, but not all, are still possible. This is the most delicious part of the design process, when the team together savors its collective and competing wishes in various forms of sketch and model.

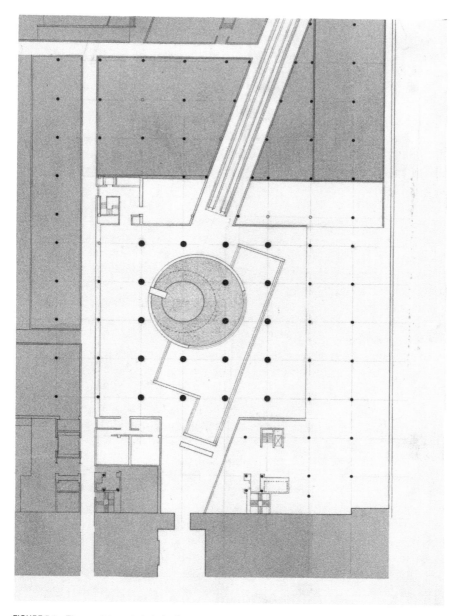

FIGURE 5.4   The persistent circle is having a difficult conversation with the columns in this undated study of the cafeteria.

The most difficult part of design isn't coming up with a good idea; the most difficult part is narrowing it to one, ruthlessly consigning all the others to a file drawer or digital folder of unfulfilled wishes.

That is what happened, apparently, to the 4th Street circle; at some point in the design process it finally rolled off the table of options, leaving a dotted trace of itself in the circle of bollards surrounding the cluster of tetrahedral skylights (see Figure 5.5). Pei did find a place for his homage, however: the circular cut in the ceiling of the lower level, allowing the visitor a glimpse of Pope's great central dome. Pei describes it: "Now we have cut an oculus in these so you can see it [the rotunda]. Before, you know, you'd come in really in the lower level, then you have to look for the stair to take you upstairs."[21] His wish for a generous opening to the sky in the connecting link instead became a window to a cascade of water. The *chadar*, as Pei calls it, may not give visitors the sky, but it offers its own drama, so close yet untouchable beyond the glass on the lower level.[22]

The site plan drawing in Figure 5.3 spells the end of the wishing; now we see the instruction for exactly how to build the plaza and skylights above the much-studied connection. Ambiguity has tapered to minimal—albeit never to none—as the drawings have shifted from wishes to instructions. As in Xeno's paradox, one never gets to a zero value of ambiguity. The interplay between certainty and tentativity in drawing media has ceased; every line, note, and dimension in a construction drawing has equal force as a jussive subjunctive, a very strong suggestion—but not an imperative—for how things ought to be executed. To ensure that Pei's dream would come true, though, the design team had to make a modal shift in their graphic language from wishing to instructing. "When we finished," said Mann, "he said his dreams had come true."[23] How did that happen?

INSTRUCTIONS

The move from wishing to instructing requires a register shift in the architect's drawings from casual, which characterize intramural design conversations, to formal, which require technical precision and adherence to accepted conventions of representation.[24] This is Act 3, when wishes become instructions, the volitional becomes jussive, and the audience itself changes. New characters—the people who will effect the translation from drawing to building—enter stage left. Except for rare exceptions,[25] the conversation about wishes is within a very different group of people than the conversation about instructions; in other words, the architect and the client talk wishes, but the architect turns to the community of builders to talk instructions. In Act 3, Carter Brown the client exits stage right, satisfied that he and Pei's team agree on their shared wish, and Pei says, in effect, "Excuse me, but I need to talk to these guys now," nodding to William Mann and his crew at Tompkins. Disney's mythology notwithstanding, simply wishing upon a star—no matter who you are—isn't sufficient. Pei himself had to do some work to make his dreams come true. He (we know it wasn't just "him"; it was "them") had to shift

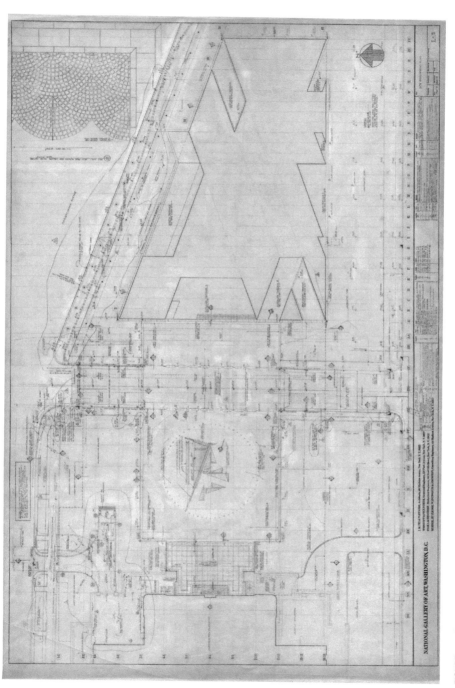

FIGURE 5.5   This site plan, more instruction than wish, shows the transmogrification of the circle into bollards.

his representational mode from wishing to instructing, and in so doing he had to turn away from his client(s) and turn toward Bill Mann. Mann is his audience now, and he's going to be instructed. On everything.

First, let's step back and regard both buildings as a pair, the West and the East Buildings of the National Gallery. Just fifty years apart in their design and construction, their respective drawings—both wishes and instructions—are as different in tenor as your language is from your grandparents'. Both the form and content of communications have changed, and continue to change as the level of what Arthur Stinchcombe calls "cognitive adequacy" continually recalibrates to align with changing practices.[26] Put simply, Stinchcombe says, "the boundaries between what is included and what excluded from the drawings or specifications are somewhat variable."[27] Cognitive adequacy describes a Goldilocks situation: when there's just enough information about the task to perform, but not so much that it belabors things. Stinchcombe, who is writing about formal systems and authority, describes cognitive adequacy as a sweet spot where accuracy, cognitive economy, and sufficiency coincide.[28] Any good set of instructions, whether to build an art museum or an IKEA bookshelf, has cognitive adequacy. Stinchcombe introduces two other concepts that characterize formal systems: "communicability," which simply means that a particular population must understand the information and the information must be transmittable, transparent, and durable; and "improvement trajectory," which means that the system must have protocols for correction and that the system itself cannot be weakened by individual circumstances. In other words, a sloppy or cognitively inadequate set of construction drawings may be a situational problem, but it doesn't invalidate the system of information known as construction drawings.

WHAT DOES THAT MEAN FOR THE CONSTRUCTION INSTRUCTIONS FOR THESE TWO BUILDINGS?

Let's look at the material they both share: stone. Pink Tennessee Marble, to be specific. If you look carefully at the columned portico of John Russell Pope's West Building, you will notice that Pink Tennessee Marble comes in a spectrum of shades and figures. The columns toward the outside are darker, announcing the ends of the portico like two exclamation points. How would the masons have known to do this? How does that wish—for two subtly darker columns in specific places—translate into cognitively adequate, communicable, and improvable instructions? Such instructions require a combination of words, numbers, depictions, and denotations across a range of media, and while the craft and techniques for articulating those instructions have changed from the 1930s to the recent renovation of the East Building in 2016, the intentions and necessity of doing so have remained the same.

The extraordinary triptych of drawings in Figures 5.6, 5.7, and 5.8, which truly deserve a chapter of their own, were produced by Malcolm Rice, the stone contractor for the Pope building; they represent the essential set of instructions explaining what kind of stone went where. We can still see the holes in the upper corners indicating that they would have been pinned to the wall of the construction office, but for "personal reference only" as the note warns. Beauty is not among the responsibilities of instructions and it can even interfere with cognitive adequacy—why is there a single scale figure, whose presence draws our mind toward *externalia* and away from our stone task?—yet even these shop drawings exude a care and craft as drawings that to modern eyes seem to exceed the information requirements. Or do they? The framing of the subject, the color pencil, the watercolor wash, together with the notes, dimensions, and lines, actually constitute a score, as if for a symphony, but it is a score for which there is only ever a single performance—the building.[29] Rice's drawings are saturated with information and a viewer can take them at a variety of semantic levels still, even as their purpose in making the building has long since been fulfilled. And yet, even after the building was complete, these drawings, like Rice himself, were not quite finished working.

Fifty years later, how did Pei convey his instructions for the stone? Remarkably, in a plot twist almost too convenient even for Shakespeare, Malcolm Rice himself was enticed out of retirement in his eighties to select the stone for the East Building. Pei knew what that would mean for his building: "He knew exactly where to get what. You see, this Tennessee Marble comes in a variety of shades. From the darkest, reddish brown, to almost white."[30] Pei is describing here in words what was so vividly represented in the drawings in the Rice triptych. Pei continues, comparing his stone challenges to Pope's:

> In the West Building, John Russell Pope, or Malcolm Rice, were able to select the marble so that for the base of the building they used dark colored stone, and then it gradually becomes lighter and lighter until it reaches the dome. That was the whitest. We tried to do the same. But we didn't have the choice. The selection was very limited by then. But we managed. We did the same thing. If you look closely you'll find we also graded our Tennessee Marble from dark to light. But not the same way; not as well as the original building. There was just not that much marble to select from.[31]

To communicate his instructions for the stone, which could almost be summarized by pointing at the older building and saying, "do it that way, as best you can," Pei and his contractor had recourse to both informal and formal information systems, to return to Stinchcombe's paradigm. They had everything that Malcolm Rice knew, not only from a lifetime in the marble business, but from his work on the very building to which Pei was adding. Pei had access to Rice's tacit "know-how"

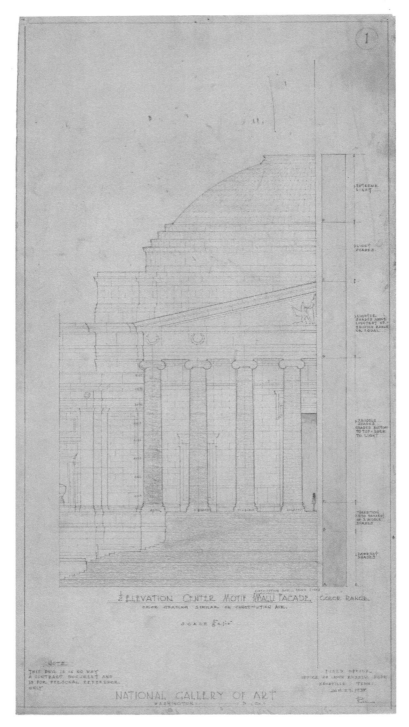

FIGURE 5.6   Malcolm Rice's three 1938 drawings: "Marble color range, half elevation, center motif of Constitution Avenue above steps and Mall façade for West Building"

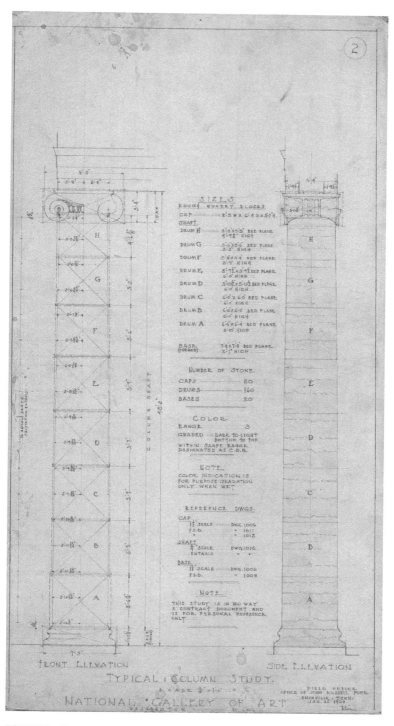

FIGURE 5.7   "Typical column study for West Building"

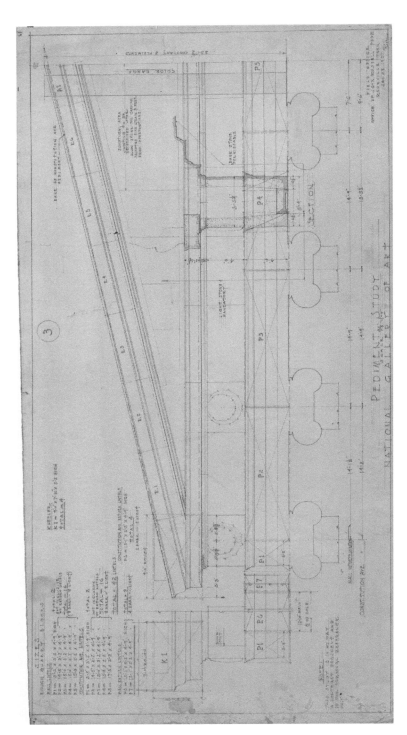

FIGURE 5.8 "Pediment study"

and to the original drawings' "know-what." Bill Mann the contractor explains, "[H]e had helpers and he'd tell them what to do, but every piece of marble was graded by Malcolm Rice and was assigned its location in the building by him."[32] This informal system was embedded in the normative formal system of the standards of construction drawings of the time. Pei's drawings therefore look very different from Rice's because, first, no one drew that way anymore, and second, because Rice's drawings continued to speak, to work. They were, and are, durable.

Pei's instruction drawings (see Figures 5.9 and 5.10) do convey the gradation of color he described, but they do so very differently from the earlier drawings. Here there is a table, or a schedule, of marble types, each keyed to individual blocks of stone in specific coursings. Where Rice used a depiction, that is, a pictorial representation, Pei's team used denotation.[33] In other words, we could—if the archivist would allow it—take one of the Malcolm Rice drawings outside, hold it up in front of the West Building's southern portico and determine its resemblances, and therefore make some assessments on whether the built work represents a faithful execution of the instructions. Does the world now indeed match this drawing? To do so requires no special key or code. We cannot do the same with Pei's drawings. Pei's stone instructions depend on deciphering where NN, PP, and so on, appear on the wall and to what type of marble those double letters refer. Sheet 809 depends on sheet 800 to be useful: sheet 800 denotes the "color coding" using a letter of the alphabet to "denote"—Goodman would be pleased—the name and shade of the marble. Sheet 800 also gives us a footprint of the building, where each stone surface has been labelled with its explicating drawing. Down in the left corner of the page—the southwest corner of the building—we see the iconic knife-edge, "drawing 809." Now we know where to look to see how the building's much-caressed corner was made: solid, "no joint." Drawing 809 concludes the stone coursing, identifying the stone from the eighth floor to the parapet. All the information we need, even where the horizontal vein turns to vertical vein, is encoded on these 800-numbered drawings. (I've only reproduced two because they really are quite repetitive; only the alphabet changes.) That is the simplest explanation of the difference between drawings that work as depictions—Rice's—and those that work as denotations. Their ends are the same, their means quite different.

Interestingly, many of Pope's—and his renderer/partner Otto Egger's—drawings for the West Building are in the Gallery's Modern Prints and Drawings collection, sharing space with Winslow Homer and James McNeill Whistler, while Pei's are in the Gallery's Archives. Both sets of drawings, whether graphite and watercolor or plastic lead on Mylar, continue to work. They have guided renovations, alterations, and maintenance of both buildings over the past nearly eighty years. Egger's meticulous interior renderings have even been used to argue that Pope intended the floors to be polished to a highly reflective finish.[34] The East Building underwent a complete renovation, which involved removing and then

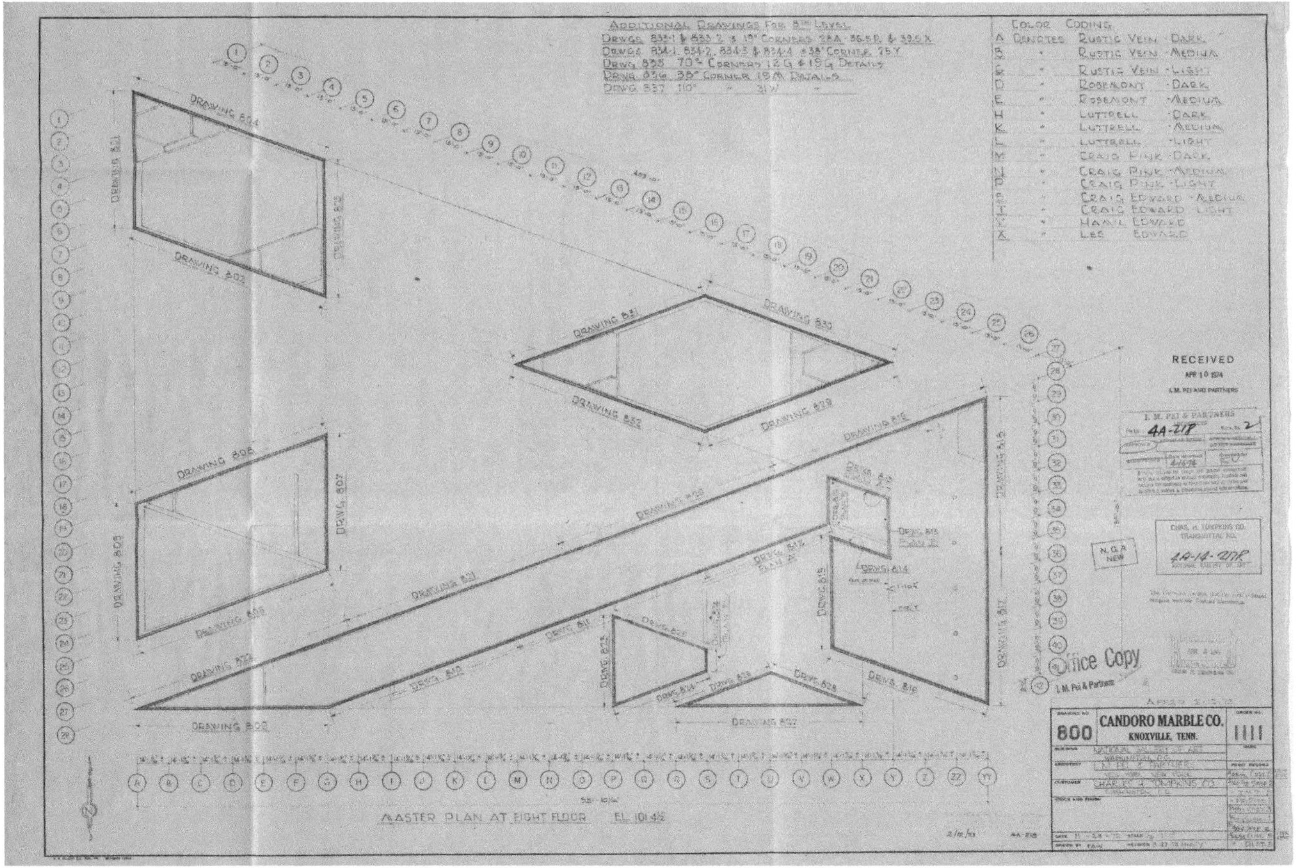

FIGURE 5.9 The stone instructions look quite different for the East Building. These 1972 drawings are from Candoro Marble: "Marble level 8, plans, elevations, and details, drawing 809"

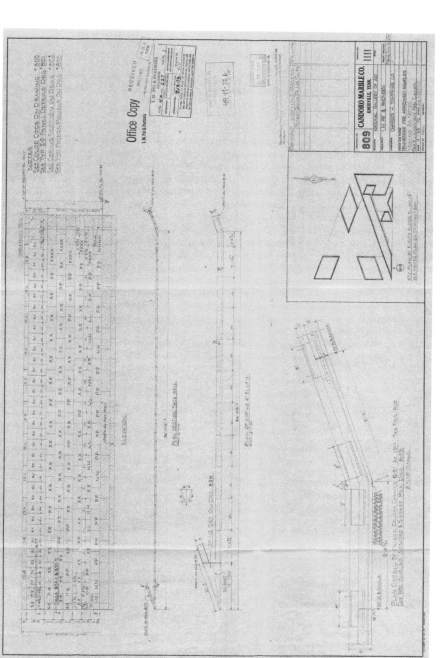

FIGURE 5.10   Candoro Marble, "Exterior marble level 8 plan, drawing 800"

reinstalling all the stone cladding in 2016. The architects referred regularly to Pei's original drawings to guide the renovation. Yet, the medium of the most recent drawings is quite different; they are entirely digital. In fact, one wonders if they are drawings at all.[35]

Construction drawings are a highly ritualized form of expression; they are formal, a word that sits at the intersection of Stinchcombe's systems theories and the scale of linguistic register. There are conventions governing the order in which drawings appear in the set, graphic conventions of dimensioning and detonating materials, and a series of orientation markers that guide the wish-fulfiller up and down a chain of construction situations from the big picture to details. There are words and numbers mixed in with drawings, as we have seen in Pope's and Pei's drawings, as is typical, and remember, there is also a companion document to the construction drawings: the specifications. Together, the "specs" and the drawings constitute the contract documents, and as such they become legal documents, with all the attendant responsibilities.

The specs speak in their own linguistic register, which is, if not completely frozen, at least slushy. The characteristic phrase is "the Contractor shall…" and from there follows a litany of things for which the Contractor is responsible. This grammatical construction (pun unintended) is called a performative, which is a statement that becomes a promise by uttering and, as you know by now, it is in the subjunctive mode. To say "the Contractor will … " does not have the same force; it is merely a prediction about the future, absent the deontic lean toward required action. It is the verb—the distinction between "will" and "shall" in this use—that determines the locutionary force of the utterance. But what about the subject of the sentence, "the Contractor?" S/he is a third person, not necessarily even known to the architect when the specs and drawings are completed. Technically then, even as I've made much over Bill Mann's role in realizing Pei's dreams, it is to a category of audience rather than a specific person or group to which the instructions are directed. The Contractor shall make the dreams of the architect come true. This is a jussive subjunctive, a mode walking right up to the edge of the imperative, but staying just to the polite side of "Hey you, make my dreams come true."

We can't conclude the section on instructions without asking, as we hinted in Chapter 3, if there is a true imperative in architectural drawing or if we only ever get to the jussive subjunctive, the *strong* suggestion. Is there some way to tell? Whether you are assembling your IKEA bookshelf or trying to figure out how to use a piece of equipment, you confront the same questions of translation and the same generosity/specificity dilemma. IKEA furniture represents the classic "kit of parts," which is a package of parts or elements and a set of specific rules governing their assembly. These instructions, particularly the post-literate pictographs of IKEA, may be the closest we come to imperative drawings. In contrast to the grab bag of wishing, praying, nudging, and musing that characterizes the subjunctive, imperatives are a tightly restricted form of directive. They are orders directed to a known but unnamed "you," that is, the second person. In the (book) case of IKEA, the "you" is, well, you, the shelf-deficient consumer.

One need not be an institutional client or the director of a museum to have wrestled with graphic instructions and their not-always-predictable conditions of satisfaction. Imagine that you have an old brick wall surrounding your garden, part of which collapsed some years ago, and the remaining section of which is missing a few bricks from the top. You need a mason to do two things: repair the section with the missing bricks and build a new section to replace the collapsed portion. How do you explain what needs to be done? You might invite the mason over, and walk around with him, pointing out everything that needs to be done, the repair and replacement. If he's meticulous, he takes notes, measurements, and photos; if he's not, he nods as if paying attention and you nod marveling at what a memory he must have. You could, if you can, draw what you want done. You could also take photos and mark the necessary work with arrows, circles, and notes. You can point to the empty space where the wall is missing and direct him either to "make it *look like* the rest of the wall" or "*build it like* the rest of the wall" and you will soon find out the difference between those two instructions. Both of these sentences are imperatives, because you are communicating to a known second person who in turn knows he is on the receiving end. But is the order clear enough to be followed? And is that really how we should speak to someone who is making our wishes come true? In all these instances though, you'll be wrestling directly with Stinchcombe's cognitive economy, which involves getting people to do what needs to be done, accurately and sufficiently. This kind of instructing and delegating is not easy, which you know intuitively if you've ever fumed that it might be easier simply to do it yourself.

The imperative, at its core, has no space for the counteroffer: the submariner who shouts "dive" is not seeking input on the means and methods of the dive, or any discussion on alternatives. Nor is your charmingly named bookshelf. Your mason, however, has a name and he probably knows more about masonry than you do, which is why you have hired him. So, as imperative as your instructions might seem, they are effectively jussives because of the knowledge imbalance between the two of you. The imperative is that locutionary point where all generosity of interpretation has burned off, leaving only extreme specificity. Trying to eke out a measure of generosity in a kit of parts can be an exercise in either frustration or creativity. In fact, you can make a conscious decision to ignore a set of instructions, as long you know the consequences, and there is educational value in trying. Rejecting instructions can be a productive exercise in foregrounding the design decisions that are latent in the instructions themselves. When I was teaching beginning design students, I regularly borrowed an assignment from legendary design educator J. Thomas Regan: students would be sent to the hobby store to purchase a model—of a plane, ship, or car, whatever—then told to throw away the instructions and build something else (see Figure 5.11). Ultimately, no matter the

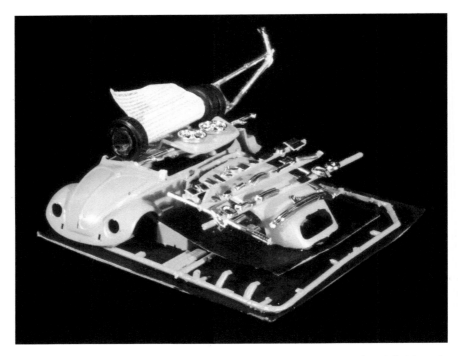

FIGURE 5.11   How not to build a Volkswagen—a beginning architecture student creatively defied the package instructions and built a typewriter.

scale or complexity of the project, the instruction game depends on the instructor and the instructee having a sufficiently shared language that their communication is effective and efficient.

That said, a cognitively sufficient set of instructions is no guarantee that one's wishes will come true. Not every project has the grand alignment of architect, contractor, client, and funding that the National Gallery has had over its life. Many architectural dreams will always live only in the parallel universe of the imagination, where the unbuilt works of students, un-premiated competition entries, recession casualties, and theoretical works sit side by side on possible sites. All design drawings are counterfactuals until they are built and they represent the same dilemma that the volitional subjunctive represents relative to futurity: the fact that something may happen or may not does not undermine the internal consistency and clarity of the wish for it to happen. Our first problem as architects is making our ideas *clear*, and determining to whom we must make them clear; the second is the more restricted problem of just *making* our ideas, and how to enlist others to do so well. This long subjunctive drama, this collective effort to make the world match the drawings, to make the wishes come true, requires an extraordinary faith in those who are the translators. What could possibly go wrong?

NOTES

1. From interviews conducted by Anne Ritchie, archivist of the National Gallery. Interview with Bill Mann, P 17.
2. Ibid, Interview with J. Carter Brown, P 1.
3. There is much more to this story—ambition, politics, power, art, and architecture—which comes through clearly in Brown's conversation with Ritchie but I've had to abbreviate it severely here, making it seem deceptively effortless.
4. Ibid, P 9.
5. Ibid, Interview with J. Carter Brown, P 2.
6. Berk, *English Syntax*, P 134.
7. Ibid.
8. *The Architecture Student's Handbook of Professional Practice*, P 244.
9. You may remember that we discussed the phases of a project in Chapter 3, "Direction of Fit," but we only mentioned the first three to avoid complicating things too soon. Now it's time for complications.
10. Interesting that we use that word—"draft"—in this sense as well as to describe the craft of precise drawing.
11. AIA Document B1012007.
12. Ibid.
13. Goodman, *Languages of Art* p 56.
14. Interview, P 43.
15. Weymouth's sketchbooks in the archives of the National Gallery, P 3.
16. Interview, P 7.
17. A "Nolli" is a type of figure–ground, named for Giambattista Nolli who produced an iconic ichnography of Rome in the middle of the nineteenth century. Its power lies in the representation of significant interior spaces and their connection to exterior spaces. The circular room of the Pantheon is shown in relation to its namesake piazza, for example.
18. Designers of a certain age will remember applying Pantone, or its black-and-white-patterned cousin Zipatone, to drawings. One would lightly lay down the entire translucent, sticky sheet and cut gently through the film along the required profile lines, then remove the excess film. There was always the risk of cutting clean through the vellum or Mylar base with your X-acto; drawing with a knife is dangerous.
19. A wish for a sidewalk café where no sidewalk exists is an example of an idle wish, a dangerous volitional subspecies for architecture. An idle wish is one that may be entertaining, but has no foreseeable path to fruition. *Exemplum gratia*: I wish I were tall.
20. Pliny thinks there's something about being able to see the process of creation:

    It is also a very unusual and memorable fact that the last works of artists and their unfinished pictures...are more admired than those which they finished, because in them are seen the preliminary drawings left visible and the artist's actual thoughts, and in the midst of approval's beguilement we feel regret that the artist's hand while engaged in the work was removed by death.

    (Pliny, XXXV, P 145.)
21. Interview, P 35–36.

22.

> The water would drop down the *chadar*, we call it. The *chadar* is really a Persian word, *chardah*. *Chardah* means a tilted plane which the water falls down on; cascades down. Many Persian gardens have that; or Islamic gardens, I think.
>
> Pei, interview, P 42. The two slightly different spellings of the word are in the original.

23. Interview, Mann, P 18.
24. What happened to the consultative register? you may be wondering. We'll talk more about that one in the following chapter, when we look at the give and take of speaking to the client and community, and all the hilarity that can ensue.
25. In the practice of hands-on design-build, the distinction between these categories is much fuzzier. There are a few interesting books on such practice, which has often been relegated to the margins of the profession of architecture. My first book, *Devil's Workshop: 25 Years of Jersey Devil Architecture*, put this kind of practice in context.
26. Stinchcombe, *When Formality Works*, P 20.
27. Ibid, P 60.
28. Ibid. He didn't actually use the words "sweet spot," or "Goldilocks." That's my interpretation.
29. Another of my oversimplifications of Nelson Goodman's representational taxonomies. Read *Languages of Art* if you're curious. See this on P 219: "Thus although a drawing often counts as a sketch, and a measurement in numerals as a script, the particular selection of drawing and numerals in an architectural plan counts as a digital diagram and as a score."
30. Interview, P 22.
31. Ibid, P 23.
32. Mann, Interview, P 43.
33. Again, see Nelson Goodman's *Languages of Art* for a fine-grained disquisition on these two representational modes, plus descriptions.
34. A long-time Gallery staffer told me this story.
35. That wondering will be postponed until the conclusion.

CHAPTER 6
THE ELEVATION: THE WORLD'S MOST DANGEROUS DRAWING

We've talked about matching the world with indicative drawings and making the world match our wishes and instructions as two flavors of subjunctive drawings, and we've talked about the latter's two different audiences of client and builder. There are, however, far more people than only the bill-paying clients straining for a peek at the wishes. These people comprise an inadvertent audience who suddenly see the curtain rise on a drama they didn't know was starting and for which they did not purchase a ticket. Let's eavesdrop on a public meeting to see how one of those audiences responds when an architect and his client share their wishes.

Once upon a time...an architect is standing at a lectern facing a group of citizens who are wary of a new project. Fliers about the meeting have been taped on the neighborhood light poles and spread through listservs. The audience, neighbors in a staid and stable corner of the city, do not appear persuaded, much less charmed, by the architect or the material he has lugged with him. They have left the torches and pitchforks outside for the time being, but they are in an aggressive posture. They are anxious about the usual things—the agony of construction, the influx of strangers and their cars, the loss of parking spaces and trees—but they are most anxious to see what the new project *looks like*.

The architect has brought sets of drawings printed at the awkward ledger size, 11x17, to hand out so everyone can follow along as he presents the project. This, however, is an unusually large crowd—see "fliers and listservs"—for a neighborhood meeting and there are not enough packets for everyone. As he speaks, people look over one another's shoulders, clumsily flipping through the floppy pages, which include a summary of the relevant zoning, the plat plan, a site plan, a set of elevations, and all of the building floor plans from garage to penthouse[1] of the nine-unit condominium. With this shaky start it appears that this will not go well. Nothing shakes up a neighborhood quite like a new project.

Ah, a new project. We use that word "project,"—*noun*, accent on the first syllable —so often that we skate over its root meaning. In his essays in *Interpretation Theory*, Paul Ricoeur pulls the word apart to reveal its origin in discourse: "that what we understand first in a discourse is not another person, but a 'pro-ject', that is, the outline of a new way of being in the world."[2] While Ricoeur claims that only writing has the power to project—*verb*, accent on the second syllable—an alternative world, it should be clear by now that architectural drawing possesses that power as well. In fact, like an inexperienced rider on a spirited horse, architects who underestimate or fail to harness that power of projection can find their projects running off out of their control. Turns out, not everyone wants a new way of being in the world; not everyone wants *this* particular new way of being. Everything depends on exactly how the architect pro*jects*—*verb*, accent on the second syllable—and tosses forward to his audience the images that depict and describe the project.

Meanwhile, back in the meeting: a citizen in the audience offers his opinion, "The design seems so insensitive to the block, to the entire area. I haven't seen a house that looks this way anywhere around here." (We'll ignore the fact that this is not a house.) Another asks acidly, "Have you done a more traditional version of this?"

Most of the comments are about the drawings labelled "elevations," particularly the one facing the street, because that is the aspect of the project that all the neighbors will have to look at daily. Buildings may legally be the property of others, but their presence is radically public, which is why these people feel that the design of this building is actually their business. The front elevation, the public side of this private building, appears several times in the set of drawings: at two different scales between its two neighboring buildings, and then at a smaller scale shown in the context of the entire block.[3] The neighboring buildings have also been drawn in elevation, with the result that their decades-old weathered brick and worn stone edges have been sharpened to hard perfect lines. The architect has made an interesting decision to produce indicative drawings of the existing buildings instead of using photographs collaged with the drawing. This reduction of the three-dimensional material world into line drawings has the effect of making the robust and thickly detailed neighboring buildings look just as flat and amaterial as the proposed building. This is always a difficult choice: the context is alive in the real world while the new project hovers in a possible world. In making this argument for the project's existence, the architects have to choose which world to share for rhetorical purposes. In this case, they have chosen to transform the real into the drawn. (We'll discuss the other option, photorealism, and its consequences, in the next chapter.) Bringing the real world across the border into the design world in this way can be a productive strategy in evaluating context and isolating variables. It's similar to a piano reduction of a symphony, which reveals essential characteristics but makes no pretense at representing the full work. Therein lies the danger.

Like composers of symphonies listening to a piano reduction, architects can make the mental translation from the real to the reduced, from the built to the drawn, and back, because the elevation offers sufficient data points to allow us to visualize how it would be if it were real. If I know that Building A, which sits to the east of the project, is brick, and that the elevation represents its brick in a certain way, then when I see that representational language on the conjectural elevation I can imagine the reality of the intended wall. If this real stuff looks like this in a drawing, then this similar drawing will look like similar real stuff. It should be a commutative resemblance, working in both directions of fit, but it works only with great effort on the part of the viewer, even visual thinkers.

Another helpful comment from the audience: "Why are you using these colors of brick? It gives a Howard Johnsons look." Ouch. The architect's non-answer—"They're Pantone colors" —does little to mollify the questioner.

Elevations, the problematic drawing here, are examples of what Goodman calls a notational language, which is one that establishes a relationship with a referent, or a compliant.[4] Every line, color, and mark in an elevation drawing *denotes* something. What makes reading such a drawing so difficult, however, is that each of those same lines, colors, and marks also seems to *depict* something. A sufficient number of lines, colors, and marks map from drawing to world that the elevation *appears* to be a depiction, but it's not. As in Malcolm Rice's stone shop drawings, both representational languages—denotation and depiction—are at play. Goodman makes the case that there is a significant difference between the two—and we deployed this pair in the previous chapter—but there might be times we mistake one for the other. And that is the case with elevations. The elevation can look an awful lot—emphasis on "awful"—like the possible building, but that is not its intention, a fact that architects can easily lose sight of. As Paul Ricoeur puts it, "denotation is a sign-thing relation,"[5] which is not the same as a resemblance. In this case, the sign is a line on paper and the thing is a bed of mortar, the edge of a cornice, or any number of possible things. Denotation, not depiction, is job number one for elevations, yet they are too often drafted into service as depictions, resulting in completely predictable misunderstandings.

What we have here, again, is the proverbial failure to communicate. Architects bear some responsibility for this failure, as we regularly speak to the public in the same words and graphic languages in which we speak to one another. We sometimes speak—as do our drawings—in the casual register, as if we're talking with our project team members, when we should be making the effort to speak consultatively, gently touching the metaphorical elbow of our audience, and guiding them through the garden of jargon. Our audience is not blameless, but we have done little to help them develop graphic literacy, or "graphicy."[6]

The public has come to this meeting to see what the project will look like. That's what those impacted by a project are most interested in, followed closely by their hallucinations of the apocalyptic traffic and undesirable populations that always accompany new projects. It is a reaction as old as history: "[E]ach man" says Aristotle "is predisposed, by the emotion now controlling him, to his own particular anger."[7] The elevation, then, *seems* to answer that question—what will it look like?—because it *seems* to resemble a building. Observers can discern doors, windows, chimneys...all the elements they know to belong to buildings. It is literally realistic, except for one thing: the conventions of perspective do not apply. This odd property makes it difficult for a viewer to determine which elements are near and which are far, which things will be visible from the street and which won't. So what exactly is an elevation, and what work does it do that can be sufficiently useful to outweigh the trouble it causes?

The typical set of architectural drawings traditionally has included plans, sections and elevations, each of which is defined as a parallel, orthographic projection of an imagined three-dimensional thing onto a two-dimensional world.[8] For the elevation, that means that each of the infinite number of points on the southern faces and edges of the imagined building, in our example, is projected perpendicularly onto a hypothetical picture plane. It's hard to envision it, because to draw an elevation one must disable the perspective instinct. Let's bring Mr. Pei back into the discussion: Figure 6.1 is an elevation of the west side of the East Building. We know from the plan and from the experience of the building that visitors enter the building through a deep porch and, furthermore, that the sides of the two towers flanking the entrance angle away toward the east. This elevation drawing, however, is not intended to depict what the building looks like, but rather denote the elements out of which it is constructed. The porch, or "entrance terrace" as it is called on the site plan (see Chapter 5, Figure 5.5) takes several paces to traverse from west to east but here it appears depthless, clinging to the surface of this drawing as if it were in the same plane as the stone wall. The exemplary concrete work, carefully selected stone, and monumental glass entry are reduced to a few banal notes: "GLASS W/ METAL MULLIONS,"—a note that could describe the entrance to a suburban Walmart—"MARBLE," and the barely cognitively adequate "ARCH CONC. HORIZONTAL BD FORM. LIGHT SANDBLAST." These notes are not the primary descriptions; those, as we've seen, are found on other sheets of drawings specifically dedicated to those specific areas. They are instead hints of how to read this otherwise austere drawing, the barest minimum of cognitive sufficiency.

One of the graphic nods to spatial depth in an elevation is often a change of line weight—how dark or light a line is—or dropping out details to indicate that something is farther away. In Pei's elevation, every joint—horizontal and vertical—in the stone is drawn on the building face to which we are supposed to direct our attention. In a graphic polysyndeton, this surface says, "This stone is like this stone

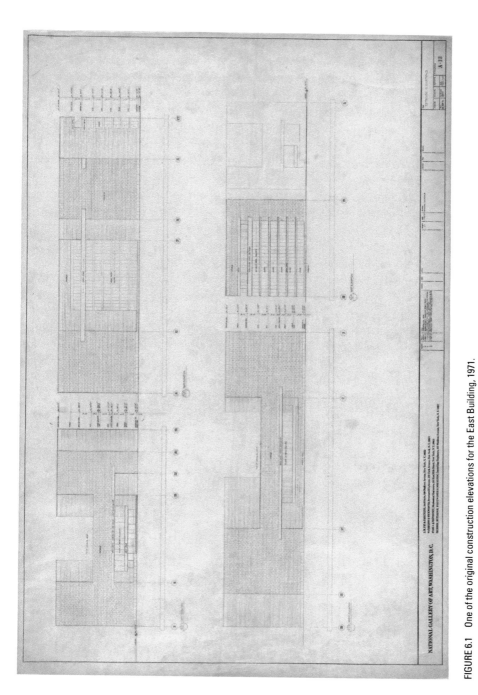

FIGURE 6.1   One of the original construction elevations for the East Building, 1971.

and this stone and this stone and this stone…" The stone cladding on the surfaces not parallel to the drawing surface only show their horizontal joints; in graphic asyndeton, they are missing their vertical joints.[9] Excessive information about material and its proper dimension and placement occupies the surface being "elevated," while information is dropped from the other surfaces, as if to say, "Look for this information elsewhere." Was it necessary to draw every single vertical joint, except insofar as it helps distinguish the primary façade from the adjacent ones? In Chapter 4, we discussed the indicative elevation of the Lockkeeper's House, where not even the horizontal joints were completely drawn. One could argue that the Lockkeeper's House is insufficiently drawn, as each of its stones would have been individually cut and each is different, whereas Pei's stone has been machine cut and has a predictable uniform dimension. Each of these drawings, however, has a different relation to the world—the Lockkeeper's elevation is indicative and the East Building elevation is a jussive subjunctive.

Learning to see in elevation, to disable the perspective instinct, takes effort. It is surprisingly difficult for beginning architecture students, who can't quite grasp that a curved space, like a bay window bulging forward from the front wall, appears in the elevation as nothing but straight lines. Elevations don't inhabit the world we inhabit. They exist as their perfect projective selves, blithely indifferent to anyone's understanding of them. There's no point of view, no space, in an elevation. Those qualities are reserved for other types of parallel projections, such as axonometrics and isometrics, and for perspectives, which are not parallel projections at all (see Figure 6.2). In the latter, things are distorted as the price paid

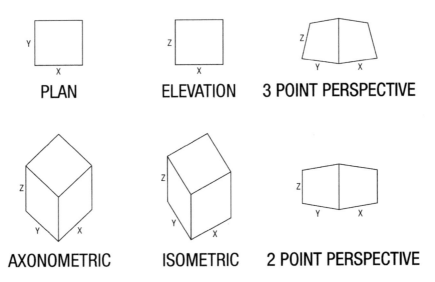

PLAN   ELEVATION   3 POINT PERSPECTIVE

AXONOMETRIC   ISOMETRIC   2 POINT PERSPECTIVE

FIGURE 6.2   A succinct summary of drawing types and projections.

for the illusion of space; in the former, the illusion of space is sacrificed for true measure and shape.[10] One way to learn how to see this flattened world is to draw existing buildings, like the Lockkeeper's House, in elevation. We know the house has a roof pitched back from the picture plane and that the dormers stand proud, yet in the elevation, the line weight of the peak is identical to that of the eave, as if the building were flattened folded paper, like a pop-up greeting card.

John Russell Pope, like many of his contemporaries, traveled the great cities of Europe to learn about architecture by drawing, and in the process learn about drawing itself. Young Pope titles the meticulous drawing in Figure 6.3 "Siena Brickwork"; it is "drawn to scale 3/8" = 1 foot" and the building is, if we trust his note, one by Renaissance master Baldassare Peruzzi. The labor required to translate the real three-dimensional world into the flatness of an elevation shows in his lines and notes. There is a note giving the dimension of the bricks on the first story, which tells us that those are the bricks he could reach to measure, and that the accuracy of the scale is dependent on his counting bricks on the upper stories. We can tell what tools he used—a straight edge, a measuring rule—to make this drawing. The elevation is unfinished, with blank areas and the now-familiar ellipses of incomplete mortar joints, as if to say "and it continues so..." but the essential information about the components, their sizes, and locations is represented, all in pure elevation. Every brick in Siena is, as is every block of stone in Washington, drawn to represent—at a designated scale—its true rather than its perceived size; they are not drawn smaller as their distance from the viewer increases. That is the distortion that Mitchell is talking about.

The same difficulty of flattening three-dimensional space applies to plans and sections, which also require conventions such as dashed lines, different line weights, and "cut lines" to telegraph space, instead of perspectival conventions. If we imagine ourselves standing in a plan, with all the walls and columns cut at about waist height, we would be able to "see" the slight perspective effect of the lines converging to the floor. Stand up, picture the room you are in sheared off like a hedge at three feet tall, look down and you'll see it. There is a vanishing point far below your feet to which all the vertical surfaces surrounding you converge. Really. That, however, is not the convention for drawing a plan; in a plan, nothing converges toward a vanishing point.[11] The data points of the wall three feet above the floor stack right above those where the bottom of the wall meets the floor; the entire wall is hidden beneath its cut line. We experience the choreography of the plan. We can grasp that different rooms are near or far from one another, and that some are larger than others, but we don't expect to see the plan laid out before us. Understanding the one-to-one notational correspondence of plan to experience is extremely difficult for laypeople, but no one expects the plan to represent what the building will look like. Sections are even more difficult for most people to understand, as they require the visualization of vertical layers of space, which do not unfold to experience the same way the plan does. In other words, it is much

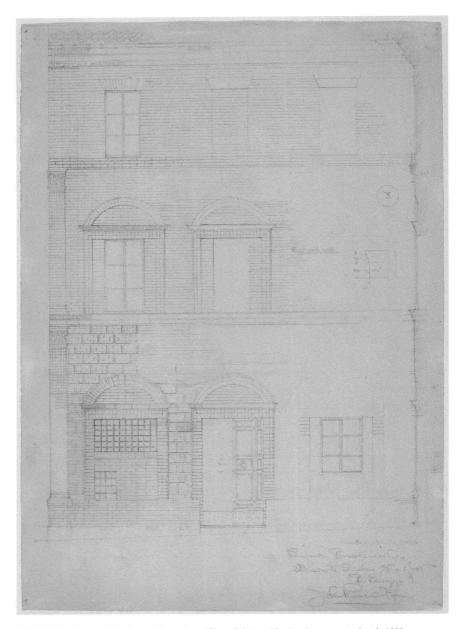

FIGURE 6.3   A young John Russell Pope drew "Siena Brickwork" when he was a student in 1896.

easier to understand the relationship of two rooms adjacent to one another in the horizontal dimension than two rooms one above the other. Even if they don't admit it—and they rarely will—people will take what they can from those two inaccessible drawings, because they don't look like buildings, but they have great expectations of the elevation and the elevation inevitably disappoints.

A drawing that uses the conventions of perspective is radically different from an orthographic projection. Western eyes have become accustomed over the centuries to understanding perspective as the key to realistic representations. In *Languages of Art* Goodman does some heavy logic-lifting to disabuse the reader of that.

> Realism is a matter not of any constant or absolute relationship between a picture and its object but of a relationship between the system of representation employed and the standard system. Most of the time, of course, the traditional system is taken as standard; and the literal or realistic or naturalistic system of representation is simply the customary one.[12]

In other words, seeing linear perspective as a "realistic" representation of the space we inhabit is simply a cultural construct, a learned paradigm. It happens, unfortunately, that the "customary one" is different for architects than for the general public. The elevation is a standard and customary way for architects to develop and assess the vertical surfaces of the building-to-be but it is not a standard or customary way for regular people to see buildings.

Let's see how our beleaguered architect and his elevations are faring...

He looks at his elevations the same way he looks at his plans: both establish relationships that will never be directly perceived by the user, but are profoundly important for the user's experience.[13] I may be generalizing, but I suspect that almost no one in the audience actually knows what an elevation is, or what the word even means in this context. Leaving aside that many people don't know which way is west unless they're out at sunset, it's probably the word "elevation" that trips them up, but no one will raise a hand in a public forum to say, "Excuse me, but what exactly is this 'elevation' of which you speak? And why does your building—soon to be our building—look so flat and unappealing?" Yet the drawing everyone has spent most of the time discussing is labeled "Proposed South Elevation."

Modernists haven't helped the case for better communications by conflating the words "façade" and "elevation" as near synonyms, but tilting toward "elevation," perhaps because the word "façade" sounds so affected and old-fashioned. Maybe it's the curly-cue under the "c" that does it; maybe it's the colloquial use of the word with its sense of well-mannered deception, as when someone adopts a polite façade toward an unwelcome interaction. Still, the distinction is not trivial: the façade is the face of the building, the manner in which it addresses the public realm. The elevation, then, is the type of drawing that denotes the facts of that face. Thus, what the unhappy assembly is actually discussing is more accurately the "Elevation of the Proposed South Façade."

There is nothing obviously dangerous or deceptive about the elevation in question. It has been drawn in color,[14] with the relentless horizontal lines of CADD-masonry—the machine never tires, unlike Pope's hand, which allowed some lines to be implied rather than drawn—and it has a title at the bottom of the sheet in large friendly letters. Unlike a real building, however, which reveals greater detail as we either move closer to it or enlist technologies like cameras or binoculars to bring it virtually closer to us, these particular elevations present the exact same information no matter which of the two scales one views. One drawing is simply printed out larger than the other; a true change of scale would be a magnification, yielding new detail and grain. Unfortunately, at whatever size, this elevation is accurate, truthful of heights, window sizes and locations, and completely uninspiring.

This is a side effect, albeit one that can be mindfully managed, of designing in digital media. Digital drawings have no scale; they are always, as my students cheerfully remind me, drawn at full scale. That presents a ridiculous problem, of course. If one were to draw absolutely everything in an elevation at full scale, the drawing would reproduce on paper as a solid black rectangle.[15] Every data point corresponding to an intended real building would be present but so densely squeezed into the miniature design world that not even light could escape. It might be more accurate to say that digital drawings problematize scale by making the "appropriate" scale of any given drawing dependent on the medium and size of its output. Thus appropriateness is impossible to achieve because modes of output are incidental and situational—tabloid-size prints for this meeting, Power Point slides for another—and design can't be framed by such future unknowns.

The by-now-exasperated architect states repeatedly in answer to comments from the audience that this is a schematic package, prepared for official "concept approval" by the Historic Preservation Review Board (HPRB) as required for any building in a historic district. "All these things are still being looked at," he says too many times to count. "What you're looking at"—he tries different words—"is a design that's still in development." Even as he is insisting that all of the lines on paper are schematic and in a state of continual change and refinement, the drawings themselves—produced using tools that have a low tolerance for ambiguity—are saying something very different: "Don't listen to him. We are measured, coordinated, and complete. We're done." Put another way, there are two components to meaning: what the speaker means, and what the sentence means. In this case, the two components are what the architect/speaker means and what the drawing means and the two here are at odds. The drawing, with lines as hard as adamantine, refuses to speak in the same conciliatory pleasantries as the architect. It's difficult to be persuasive if your own drawing is contradicting you, insisting on its completion and finality. The result is that a citizen, who has showed up to the meeting hoping to have input—in the back and forth of the consultative register, the give and take of new points of view—on an important new addition to his neighborhood instead sulks and grows more alienated and suspicious of the process. You can see how hard it is *not* to take a hardline drawing as fact, for it has reached the far end of the generosity-to-specificity spectrum. When every mortar joint in the elevation is represented in lines of *exactly* the same dimension and spaced exactly x distance apart—the computer can't help itself, this is how it rolls—the denotation and exemplification arrows are locked onto each other like guided missiles.

As if to emphasize its finality, the drawing has "call-outs," helpful notes indicating the names and materials of exactly the things about which the audience members are concerned. Noticing a written annotation on the drawing, a citizen wails, "Aluminum windows? That's like something you'd find in NoMa."[16] The architect immediately reassures the audience that the windows could just as easily be wood. Of course, they *could*, but the annotation says otherwise. There is nothing in the drawing itself that depicts aluminum, only the words "ALUM WINDOW"[17] with an arrow pointing to the windows. In the case of architectural drawings, the "arrows" of denotation and exemplification that Goodman talks about are real arrows, without quotation marks. That one note, "ALUM WINDOW," sets off a negative reaction in the audience, because an exemplification on the drawing is doing double duty as a denotation for a class of undesirable characteristics: cheapness, commercial–looking, association with other types of buildings that don't look like "our kind" of building, and so on. The architects no doubt consider that denotation as contingent, still under consideration. He is speaking honestly when he says they "could be wood windows; we haven't really decided." Meanwhile of course, the drawing stands next to him saying, "These are aluminum windows. See the arrow? Every time you see a window here, it's an exemplification of aluminum-ness. Is that clear?" That's how drawings talk when they're hard-lined.

I know—because I talked to him afterward—that the architect didn't enjoy this. He and his two colleagues left the meeting discouraged and puzzled, chalking up the lukewarm-to-hostile response to the oft-repeated truism that the general public just can't read drawings. They are, to use my invented word, "iggraphic," but that does not prevent them from having an opinion. There is such a thing as an innate ability for spatial reasoning and certain people are good at it, others not. Noted educator and writer Howard Gardner identifies spatial intelligence as one of his multiple intelligences:

> Central to spatial intelligence are the capacities to perceive the visual world accurately, to perform transformations and modifications upon one's initial perceptions, and to be able to re-create aspects of one's visual experience, even in the absence of relevant physical stimuli.[18]

Gardner raises the conventional and contentious bicameral split between visual/spatial[19] and verbal intelligences—right brain for visual/spatial, left for verbal—but even as he admits to some discomfort with such a reductive view; he accepts that most of us do sort out information that way.

Like other innate abilities, though, spatial reasoning can be learned by those who don't have it, and left unexplored by those who do. Design professionals are so accustomed to looking straight through the drawing to the drawn that it's easy to forget that it is a learned skill. Further, once learned it can never be unlearned. In the same way that we can never truly see the world as we saw it when we were children, once we have mastered a language or skill we can never see the problems of the discipline naïvely. If you read music, you can never reexperience how hard it was to learn. Consequently, people who are particularly fluent in these other unnatural languages can be brutally impatient with those who are not. Amazingly—to me at least—Gardner never mentions architecture or architects in his discussion of spatial intelligence, although he stresses that this is a valuable intelligence to possess, particularly for, say, sculptors or mathematical topologists.[20] With all due respect to topologists, it's unlikely that one has had to defend the construction of a new theorem to a group of topologically-illiterate neighbors concerned about the Klein bottles littering the neighborhood. The dilemma for architects, but not for topologists, is the disparity between their spatial intelligence and the likely spatial intelligence of their own clients, not to mention the larger public, and even, perhaps, builders.

The problem often with architectural drawings, as Goodman says relative to other representations, is that within an information-laden drawing such as an elevation many things are being exemplified—that is, "a sample and what it refers to"[21]—but there are also many things in the drawing that aren't. How is a viewer to know which things to take as exemplifications? The drawing says the windows are aluminum, although that information comes from a word not a discriminating mark, but the architect says they could be wood. The façade looks to be brick, yes, but is it necessarily that color? There is a misalignment of the generosity/specificity spectrum, with only the architect's words, spoken not drawn, serving to recalibrate the specificity of the drawings. In the case of the "Howard Johnson's"-color brick, the problem could be solved by making different decisions about what information to share or what to exemplify. The color Burnt Umber—or Howard Johnson's Umber—can be used to denote anything, for example, in a chart, map, etc., but when it's applied across the surface of a wall in an elevation and, furthermore, if that wall is marked with parallel horizontal lines, the color probably exemplifies brick, or possibly terracotta. The architect can stand next to the drawing and say whatever he wants, but the drawing is saying this will be a brick building, and the brick will be this color. Interestingly, if either of those two indicators—either the color or the horizontal lines—is *not* drawn, the denotation arrow points at several possibilities. If there is only color, we have a list of possible denotations, including painted wood, stucco, and, yes, brick or terracotta. If only the horizontal lines are present, then the color of the brick—and even if it *is* brick—remains undetermined and thus open to discussion. The seasoned architect learns to withhold certain denotations and exemplifications, not only to keep his options open but to prevent such distracting arguments in public hearings about which hotel chain the brick resembles. Consider the series of images in Figures 6.4–6.6. The first (Figure 6.4) reveals the elevation dilemma—flatness; it is clear where railings, doors, and windows are vertically, but not spatially. The second (Figure 6.5) deploys shadows to telegraph projections and recesses, casting and receiving shade from a monochrome sun. In the third image (Figure 6.6) the building finally snaps into position in recognizable, conventional, space. Only now, with this depiction, do we really understand what we have been looking at.

The architect probably did run through these exemplification options in the office, pinning up different colors for discussion within the design team, but may have decided not to open that choice to public vote. In this case, colorless brick with a note "brick color to match existing house to the west" might have made everyone in the audience happy, except those contrary few who prefer the color of the bricks on the building to the east. Why? Not necessarily because they love those bricks, but because they *know* them and in their own minds' eyes can provide the exemplification for the graphic denotation. Moreover, they can leave the meeting, walk across the street and say, "Ah, so it will look like this. How nice."

To correct the window material problem—the ALUM problem—is easier: don't name the material. This doesn't mean never to call out the material, only that naming it thus at the conceptual stage is invoking a level of specificity out of proportion to what's known about the building; it's "misspecific," another made-up word that means "specificity at the wrong time or in the wrong place." Words can outrun the drawing. Because the elevation annotated in this way is a jussive, a bit of instructing is rudely intruding on the wishes. Sharing an instruction for how to make the building, rather than a wish for how it might look once built—which is the only thing the public is justifiably interested in—in such a situation reifies urban myths about the arrogant architect who won't meet the public halfway in envisioning a possible future. In reality, it's less arrogance than amnesia, a forgetting that wishes and instructions are two very different modes of expression. Look again at I. M. Pei's elevation for the East Building, with its combination of words and lines. "GLASS W/ METAL MULLIONS" is almost as off-putting as ALUM WINDOWS, but we know that this elevation served as an instruction, a jussive subjunctive. Its audience was tightly circumscribed. Our architect is deploying the marks and conventions that are appropriate to instructions, but what is needed in this situation is the volitive subjunctive expression of a wish.

The elevation serves a crucial role in the set of drawings that comprise the instructions for building but it is fundamentally aspatial and amaterial, even though space and material are encoded therein. That code says, for example, that these lines trace the size and location of a certain type of window, specified and described elsewhere. When the staff intern adds the signifiers of reality, such as

FIGURE 6.4   A pure elevation, more denotation than depiction, can be a challenge to read. Drawing and design by Douglas R. Palladino

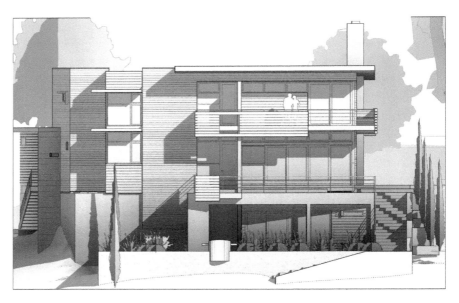

FIGURE 6.5   Add shadows, and things start to look better. Drawing and design by Douglas R. Palladino

FIGURE 6.6   The conventional and customary view—perspective—finally gives us a depiction we can place in real space. Drawing and design by Douglas R. Palladino

color, texture, and entourage—that catch-all for the life we hope will encircle and enliven our buildings—to bring some of the lived world into the drawing, she can, oddly, just make things worse.[22] The elevation, infinitely flat like something out of Edward Abbott's imagination,[23] gets decorated as if it exists in the same thick space we do, trying to be something it isn't. In this way, a drawing created originally to carry one kind of locutionary force has been repurposed for a very different kind. If a drawing is to be understood as provisional, as a draft, then the locutionary aspect of the drawing needs to support that reading (see Figure 6.7). No one would look at this drawing and take it as a final proposal. It is sufficiently anchored to a real place, thanks to effective photo-collaging, but the proposed building is still in the process of congealing into something equally solid as the surroundings. Parts of the building speak with more certainty—we see suggestive color and material textures—but other parts aren't yet even committed to a final volume. A rough sketch, an in-process hybrid such as this elevation, means something and by sharing it the architect means something; those meanings should align with one another and together be appropriate to the situation. If the situation is a public forum to discuss—in the consultative register—various options, then the drawing and the architect's words should provoke the desired action: comment, revision, development.

In his book *How to do Things with Words*, J. L. Austin warns:

Since our acts are actions, we must always remember the distinction between producing effects or consequences which are intended or

FIGURE 6.7   This hybrid elevation, a collage of photographs, digital and hand drawings, sits well to the generosity side of the spectrum. Drawing and design by Abi Kallushi

unintended; and (i) when the speaker intends to produce an effect it may nevertheless not occur, and (ii) when he does not intend to produce it or intends not to produce it, it may nevertheless occur.[24]

In other words, watch out for intended and unintended consequences and remember that there may be little correlation between what you intend to happen and what actually happens. But that shouldn't prevent us from acting. In a meeting, whether within the design team, with a client, or in public, the act can be projecting slides, or placing finished drawings on easels, or unrolling yellow trace paper, and each of these has different levels of meaning, of illocutionary force. There is the material being presented, and there is the act of how it is presented. The consultative gesture of unrolling paper on a shared table is also a performative, an act that does what it says. The propositional content of blank paper is not so blank after all.

What an audience in a design review meeting longs for are architectural drawings—or images of any sort—that can communicate the ineffable experience of a new way of being in the world, as promised by the building. How will it smell? What will the shadows of the oak tree look like playing across the brick? Will it reaffirm the way I see my neighborhood? We want to see it so we can "pro-ject" ourselves into the image and be changed. We want poetry. It's a lot to ask. One of the big difficulties in architectural drawing is the vast distance between the clarity and specificity of technical language and the ambiguity and instability of poetic language and that is precisely where the elevation's danger lies.

NOTES

1. Helpful hint to architects: "penthouse" means different things to different people. The gap between a vision of a luxury residence and the reality of a box of mechanical equipment is wide and was the source of some inadvertently comical confusion among this crowd. We need not mention what it means to certain male magazine "readers."
2. Ricoeur, *Interpretation Theory*, P 37.
3. Don't look for the drawing here; you won't find any images of this particular project. Considering how this protocol plays out it didn't seem fair to the architect, whose body of work is far better than this encounter might lead one to believe. Attend your own neighborhood NIMBY Assoc. and you can enjoy your own episode.
4. Nelson Goodman, *Languages of Art*. I've referenced this perhaps too often. It's a wonderfully original work, even if it gets kind of thick into the language of logic to explain things.
5. Ricoeur, *Interpretation Theory*, P 123.
6. Given that we have the terms "literacy" and "numeracy," we should be able to talk about "graphicy"—the ability to read drawings. We can also then coin its opposite, "iggraphicy," analogous to "illiteracy." Yes, these are new words. You may use them from now on.
7. Aristotle, *Rhetoric*, P 39.
8. Why did I use the past participle and not the present in this sentence? Because Building Information Modelling is currently problematizing what constitutes a "set" of architectural drawings. I'll raise more questions than I answer about this in Chapter 8.
9. "Polysyndeton" and "asyndeton" are two figures from classical rhetoric. The former is an excessive *and* relentless *and* repetitive use of conjunctions, while the latter is succinct, condensed, brief with none. Those are two great words and I just wanted to use them.
10. William Mitchell offers a detailed a more scholarly description of these drawings types in a section of *The Logic of Architecture* (P 65–67) titled "Conventions of Depiction." This book, along with his *The Reconfigured Eye*, is definitely worth a read if you want more depth than I've provided.
11. That said, some software, such as SketchUp, treats the building as a drawn object that is constantly in real space. Plans and sections are then the result of slicing the object and those drawings retain the perspective of that view rather than the convention of the parallel projection. This may seem like a minor difference but it is one of the marks of a generational divide in the practice of architecture. Speaking from the pre-SketchUp side of that divide, it drives me crazy.
12. Goodman, P 38.
13. One of the architects in this example provided this explanation in a discussion at his office.
14. I hesitated to say it is "drawn" in color, because it is the output of digital production. Should I say it is "put out" in color? Perhaps just "printed" in color.

15. For more—far more—on this problem see James Gleick's tome *The Information*, particularly P 384–385. He raises the dilemma of whether to "describe the whole world in all its detail" in representations, referring to Lewis Carroll's description of "the ultimate map, representing the world on a unitary scale…"

16. "NoMa" is a rapidly developing neighborhood in Washington, so named because it is NOrth of MAssachusetts and being so named lends instant hipster cache. This classist swipe, disguised as architectural critique, refers to the look of many of the area's recent residential buildings, many with aluminum details in window frames, exterior shading fins, and balcony railings.

17. The use of ALL CAPITAL LETTERS, so typical of architectural drawings, has developed a different meaning, thanks to protocols of social media and email. Now, ALL CAPS signify SHOUTING, and are considered RUDE. I worry about this.

18. Gardner, *Frames of Mind: The Theory of Multiple Intelligences*, P 173. His chapter on spatial intelligence opens with several pages of diagrams and drawings designed to test for that ability. Interestingly, it's the only chapter that actually shows the material germane to the intelligence. No score appears in the discussion of musical intelligence; no formulae for mathematical.

19. Ibid, P 177. Also, he tends to use the less sensorially biased term "spatial" over "visual," citing research showing spatial intelligence in the visually impaired.

20. Gardner, *Frames of Mind: The Theory of Multiple Intelligences*, P 190.

21. Goodman, *Languages of Art*, P 53.

22. The architect in this case lamented that "the minute we start rendering them [the elevations] they became something else."

23. Abbott's wonderfully weird story, *Flatland*…just had to reference it.

24. Austin, *How to do Things with Words*, P 106.

CHAPTER 7
INTO THE UNCANNY VALLEY

> *Thousands of square miles of polished rock with not one blade of grass, not one fibre of lichen, not one grain of dust. Not even air. Have you thought what it would be like, my friend, if you could walk on that land?*
>
> C. S. Lewis, *That Hideous Strength*

We've established that every architectural representation, whether traditional drawing, model, narrative spec, or "building information model," acts like an utterance and establishes a relationship to the world. It has a job to do and a way of working. The usefulness of these representations depends on whether that relationship is clear to the various audiences who are invested in the relationship. Ironically, the most sophisticated digital renderings, those that can ray-trace and model with the most exacting verisimilitude, can render—pun intended—that relationship problematic.

I was flipping through a glossy magazine entertaining myself with the fantasy real estate and I saw a full-page ad for one of the new "starchitect"-designed condominiums in Lower Manhattan. The image showed a dramatic view into one corner on an upper floor, from the perspective of a peeping peon looking longingly through the cruel window. Through the impossibly clear glass framed in crisp white mullions, the image revealed a granite and stainless kitchen and the obligatory black leather and chrome furniture. All was as expected until I noticed the fine print: "This is an actual photograph." Unlike the assorted lawyered-up annotations of contemporary life—professional driver, do not attempt; past performance cannot be used as guide to future performance; this page intentionally left blank, et al.—this was not a disclaimer so much as a *claimer*, a small bit of the verbal testimony required of an unreliable witness. The image was so perfect, so free of the blemishes of everyday life, that the creators of the ad feared that the image was not credible. Such perfection, the viewer would probably think, can't be real; it must be a computer rendering. As in ads for mascara, reality just can't look that good.

What are we to make of this admission, with its unwittingly Magrittean overtones? What is a prospective buyer to make of it? Are we troubled to learn that the image is an indicative photograph and not a subjunctive rendering? Or troubled because we can't tell the difference? It is disconcerting to realize that we can't quite sort out the relationship of an image to the world, like not understanding whether someone is telling you a true story or a fable. In her seminal critique of photography, Susan Sontag connects the medium's explicit struggle with veracity —photography has always manipulated the truth—to the development of techniques for retouching negatives. As she tartly puts it, "The news that the camera could lie made getting photographed much more popular."[1] More seriously, she goes on,

> The consequences of lying have to be more central for photography than they ever can be for painting, because the flat rectangular images which are photographs make a claim to be true that paintings can never make. A fake painting (one whose attribution is false) falsifies the history of art. A fake photograph (one which was been retouched or tampered with, or whose caption is false) falsifies reality.[2]

Further, an unreliable photograph also threatens the credibility of all photography and with it the entire category of indicative image production. Would that Sontag were still with us—Walter Benjamin too—to train her analytical skills on the current problematic of digital image making.[3]

But why does the distinction between the real and unreal, the true and fake, matter at all? Why does it matter to architecture? Remember that there is a real world and there is a design world. In any design proposal there is a necessary degree of overlap —technically called the "intersection" in the set theory community—between the two worlds. As in a Venn diagram (see Figure 7.1), that overlap is negotiated anew at the start of every project, and is constantly renegotiated as a project moves through its wish and instruction phases to its translation into the real world. The two sets may sit farther apart in the early wishing of a conceptual design phase and roll back together if one is fortunate enough to get to the instruction and construction phase. All the project participants together construct the degree of overlap consensually but there are certain elements of reality—gravity, for example—that simply cannot be excluded. An architect and client may decide at the start of a project to ignore some fact of the real world, such as the existence of a large tree in the middle of a site; but at some point the continuing existence of the oak might need to be weighed against the longing for a lap pool. For too long designers and clients ignored irrefutable and inconvenient environmental facts. An unshaded south-facing glass façade identical to its north-facing partner testifies to a gap—the absence of an intersection—between the real world and the design world. (In the design world, the sun rises only when

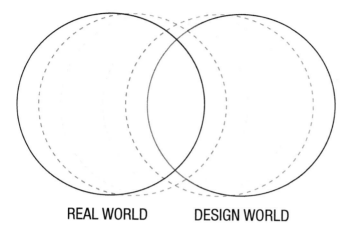

REAL WORLD   DESIGN WORLD

FIGURE 7.1   The overlap between the real world and the design world is always shifting.

and where the architect wishes.) Today the regulatory apparatus of construction specifies much of the contents of that intersection—the inviolability of emergency egress, for example—but even that has been culturally constructed over time. Before the passage of the Americans with Disabilities Act (ADA) an entire class of citizens occupied a bubble in the real world that rarely intersected with the desires of the design world.

Still, the size and contents of the intersection are renegotiated during the design process as values shift, and as facts are added, temporarily tabled, then reintroduced; but if one has designs on the real world, so to speak, then the existence of an overlap is never in question. Architecture demands an intersection, but not a total eclipse. When reality eclipses the imagination, the result is mind-numbing banality; when the imagination eclipses reality, then we have abandoned architecture for the untethered spheres of science fiction, gaming, or art. We balance at the disconcerting edge where images become ends in themselves rather than representations of a plausible new reality.[4]

The overlap, the intersection, between those worlds is fundamental to the act of design. Gradually, the circles of the two worlds roll toward one another as the design approaches a one-to-one correspondence with the real world. More and more stuff begins to occupy the intersection: stairs acquire treads and risers; doors appear with directions of swing; thicknesses of glass and window types are scheduled, names of things are called out in rude all-caps—"ALUM WINDOWS!" Still, this incremental acquisition of specificity is neither inevitable nor a natural movement.

Our representational tools now approach a truly deceptive level of verisimilitude, such that advertisements need to include fine print asserting that the accompanying image is an actual photograph. Can a drawing, a rendering, be so real that it unsettles the viewer? As readers and interpreters of the visual world, we like to think that we can discern photographs from paintings or drawings. We might marvel at the skill of the seventeenth-century Dutch painter Willem Claesz Heda, whose rendering of glass in *Still Life with Oysters* looks astonishingly real. But we are never in doubt as to whether it *is* real; we marvel because it *looks* real. Without replaying the entire history of painting in the Western world, it isn't an exaggeration to say that the quest for verisimilitude dominated painting until the camera arrived on the scene and brought that quest to a screeching halt. Yet, early photographers often adopted a painterly look for their images, borrowing conventions of composition and subject matter, even as the painters pretty much threw in the realism towel and began to recalibrate the very definition of painting.[5]

You may argue on your own time about photography's claim as art, but it is, by our definitions here, an *indicative* form of representation: it draws from the world and aims to match it. As Susan Sontag says, "The picture may distort; but there is always a presumption that something exists, or did exist, which is like what's in the picture."[6] The small-print "claimer" at the bottom of the real estate ad suggests that in an age of digital representation such a presumption has been thrown into question. What relationship with the world do you intend with this work—matching the world or making the world match it? Today that very presumption is in doubt. Contemporary technologies—digital drawing and modeling, digital collage, and photo-editing software such as Photoshop—are blurring the old boundaries in ways that would have been impossible in the era of mechanical mockups. Photographs look like digital renderings; digital renderings look like photographs. This representational chiasmus leaves a viewer puzzled about the very intentions of an image. We do not know what we are looking at, or how to evaluate it. Is it real or not? An image that needs a qualifier, an extra-graphic annotation, to establish its relationship to the world is an image slipping downslope into what the roboticist Masahiro Mori calls the "uncanny valley."

Mori introduced the concept of the uncanny valley in 1970, in a brief essay in *Energy*, an in-house magazine for Esso (now Exxon).[7] Mori described his research into the ways in which humans respond to robots and he identified a curious and complicated phenomenon. Up to a point, he found, anthropomorphic qualities in robots provoked positive responses; as the robots appeared more human-like, people found them more appealing. At some tipping point of anthropomorphism— say, somewhere between C-3PO and Ava from *Ex Machina*—the robots became disconcerting. Mori offers as an example the invention of increasingly sophisticated prosthetics.

Recently, owing to great advances in fabrication technology, we cannot distinguish at a glance a prosthetic hand from a real one. Some models simulate wrinkles, veins, fingernails, and even fingerprints. Though similar to a real hand, the prosthetic hand's color is pinker, as if it had just come out of the bath. One might say that the prosthetic hand has achieved a degree of resemblance to the human form, perhaps on a par with false teeth. However, when we realize the hand, which at first sight looked real, is in fact artificial, we experience an eerie sensation. For example, we could be startled during a handshake by its limp boneless grip together with its texture and coldness. When this happens, we lose our sense of affinity, and the hand becomes uncanny.[8]

The metaphoric "valley" is the dip in Mori's graph (see Figure 7.2), the point at which human-like robots lose their charm and become repellant. Mori acknowledged in a 2011 interview with *Wired* that his theory originated in his own quirky views on robots, toys, and life-like figures. He recalled his uncomfortable reaction as a child to wax figures in exhibition dioramas and how years later, when he was a professor at the Tokyo Institute of Technology, those memories informed his work with robots.

You know those wax dolls at exhibition halls? Like Columbus discovering America? I never really liked those. When I started working with robots,

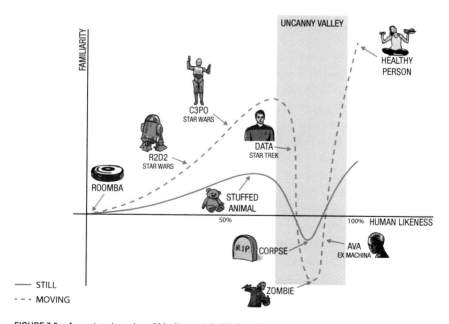

FIGURE 7.2   An updated version of Mori's graph by Marium Rahman.

I remembered those dolls, and I thought, wouldn't it be creepy if there was a human who didn't blink? If their eyes just stared and stared at you...[9]

Creepy indeed. Mori's uncanny valley steepens and deepens when the robot possesses the possibility of movement. He draws a distinction between industrial robots, which are mere machines with no intended life-like qualities, and toys, the success of which often depends upon anthropomorphism. A machine that moves and then stops, he explains, is simply a stopped machine; its limited movements mean nothing. For a life-like robot, on the other hand, both movement and stillness are problematic: either its movements are insufficiently human and therefore cause unease or its stillness is a kind of death. In his *Energy* essay, Mori discusses a "highly sophisticated" robot that was constructed for the 1970 World Exposition in Osaka. To enable it to smile, the robot was designed with "29 pairs of artificial facial muscles in the face (the same number as a human being)." The robot, however, could not laugh at the same speed as the humans, making it seem not happy but "creepy." "This shows how," Mori continues, "because of a variation in movement, something that has come to appear very close to human—like a robot, puppet, or prosthetic hand —could easily tumble down into the uncanny valley."[10]

For many years Mori's research remained obscure; only recently, as new technologies in the film and gaming industries began eroding the bounds between live-action and cartoon animation, have his insights begun to attract attention. To "animate" is to give or bestow spirit or life, to make something quite literally come alive. When that gift is bestowed on the inanimate—toys, for example—the result can be charming. Pixar has made a fortune by animating things, such as an implausibly charming Luxo light.[11] However, when the *already*-animate is animated the results range from awkward to grotesque and even frightening.[12] In Pixar's famous *Toy Story*, the animated toys draw the viewer into a state of magical delight. (Freud—whose own take on the uncanny we will get to shortly—would no doubt add that this is because all sorts of repressed memories are returning to our conscious minds, and he may be right, but let's leave it at delight.) The children and adult characters, however, seem *de*-humanized through animation. In particular their movements—especially gravity-related movement such as running or jumping—seem inauthentic and disturbing; *creepy*, as Mori might put it. We have no way of assessing the realism of Mr. Potato Head's gait, but we do know what a running child should look like, and so we are unsettled when we see that the animation is out of phase with real motion.[13]

Because the experience of the uncanny arises in that perceptual space between a thing and a mind, it was of keen interest to Sigmund Freud, even as he admitted that it might seem an odd subject for a psychoanalyst.[14] In his influential essay on the subject, he describes the uncanny as "that class of the terrifying which leads back to something long known to us, once very familiar."[15] He uses the German terms *"heimlich"* and *"unheimlich,"* first emphasizing their opposite meanings of "familiar" and "unfamiliar"; but then, as if entering an infinity of mirrors, he argues that the differences start to collapse as what is known begins to seem strange, and as what is unfamiliar appears to be known.[16]

Architectural representations often embody this tension between familiar and unfamiliar. In an effective rendering, new buildings or landscapes share the same illusionistic space with images of existing buildings or landscapes. As we have discussed, adept users of Photoshop can achieve a level of exquisite confusion between the real and the unreal unimaginable in the old days of cutting and pasting.[17] *Haven't we seen this place before?* Subjunctive representations are already perilously close to the edge in their depiction of things that don't yet exist but that look as if they do...or could. It is at once known and strange, familiar and unfamiliar, *heimlich* und *unheimlich*.

Here it is useful to remember that the primary purpose of making an architectural drawing is *not* to induce an aesthetic experience; not to create a composition to be evaluated relative to a framed picture-space. In *Languages of Art*, Goodman provides a succinct list of characteristics that distinguish the aesthetic from the non-aesthetic: "Density, repleteness, and exemplificationality, then, are earmarks of the aesthetic; articulateness, attenuation, and denotationality, earmarks of the nonaesthetic."[18] Members of the viewing public, whether paying clients or impacted citizens, do not contemplate architectural representations with aesthetic detachment. We look *into* them—*through* them even more than *at* them—to divine possible futures. Yet, often the experience *feels* aesthetic. What is problematic is our confusion as to the object of that experience: is it the building or the image of building? That confusion can lead to making architectural decisions based on a seductive and potentially deceptive image. "An uncanny effect," Freud writes,

> is often and easily produced by effacing the distinction between imagination and reality, such as when something that we have hitherto regarded as imaginary appears before us in reality, or when a symbol takes over the full functions and significance of the thing it symbolizes.[19]

What are some specific tells of uncanniness in architectural drawing? We'll touch on three of them here: conventions of perspective space, which we touched on in the last chapter, representations of humans, and stairs. These three are among the most familiar/unfamiliar components of our lived worlds, so they make good uncanny candidates. When they are re-presented to us in ways that blur the imagination/reality boundary, or unsettle our understanding of the image in other ways, they become our escorts into the valley.

PERSPECTIVE

In *That Hideous Strength*, the final book of his dystopian space trilogy, C. S. Lewis describes hell as a place where perspective space breaks down.[20] He writes of the chilling experience of his protagonist, Mark, in a kind of futuristic captivity:

> Sitting staring about him he next noticed the door—and thought at first that he was the victim of some optical illusion. It took him quite a long time to prove to himself that he was not. The point of the arch was not in the centre: the whole thing was lopsided. Once again, the error was not gross. The thing was near enough to the truth to deceive you for a moment and to go on teasing the mind even after the deception had been unmasked. Involuntarily one kept shifting the head to find positions from which it would look right after all.[21]

For Lewis's hero, the experience of the *heimlich* and *unheimlich* in such close correspondence constituted damnation. These "not gross" errors are pervasive in hand-drawn perspectives, especially among novices as they struggle to get the objects they see in space to conform to the rules of perspective. It is much harder than it looks because a perspective drawing of the world done correctly appears effortless. Is it because we are awash in utterly convincing perspectival images through the ubiquity of the photograph—magnified logarithmically since the rise of camera capabilities in mobile phones—that we continue to accept geometric perspective as *the way the world looks*? No matter the massive democratization of the means of image production, it's that old, privileged view that remains the dominant mode, or at least the default. Think of how the holodeck in *Star Trek* is represented before the program is activated: a fully Cartesian grid, the Federation Starship as if envisioned by Alberti.

We accept linear perspective as the way the world looks, still clinging to a fifteenth century paradigm for representing the world and proud that our twenty-first century software has perfected it. Nonetheless art historians have long debated whether linear perspective was a discovery or an invention—a depiction of the truth of the world or an ingenious visual convention.[22] Where are the time–space complexities of Cubism, the atmospheric luminosity of the Impressionists, in our contemporary ways for representing the possible world? Paul Cezanne flouted the rules, yet his paintings of landscapes present the world as experienced, with multiple, non-intersecting planes, softened edges and blue distances. His paintings match the world sufficiently that we can recognize the mountain and mentally inhabit the landscape even if we can't measure it.

Brunelleschi's famous demonstration at the Baptistery produced an awe-inspiring—*mirabile visu*—indicative drawing, an unprecedented act of world-matching. Underlying it were the rules that allowed the direction of fit to run in both directions with equal plausibility. Robin Evans observes in *The Projective Cast*, with some surprise and a whiff of disdain, that after Brunelleschi showed his peers how to draw the real world convincingly, it appears very few painters cared to do so. Instead, they all used his method to produce "inventions and fantasies" in which the architecture—designed in perspective-friendly straight lines—was "less well connected to the existing world…than were the figures, because the figures, though largely inventions, were based closely on observed studies from life, whereas most of the architecture was not."[23] Evans argues that the architecture came from the painters' imaginations and from the rules of perspective—technique shaped its manifestation. This is very different, however, from using the technique with the intention of bringing that imagined piece of architecture into the existing world. (As for the "figures," we'll get to them later.)

The conflation of painting and photography as ways of representing the world suggests one of the sources of tension—of the uncanny—in hyper-realistic digital renderings. To put it another way: is an architectural rendering more akin to a painting or a photograph? Again, as Sontag reminds us, we understand a photograph to be *of* something that did or does exist, no matter what lens, filters, or films were deployed to transform it. A painting has no necessary connection to the real, as Goodman's centaur problem suggests. Before digital technologies, architectural renderings were more akin to, and in fact often were, paintings. It was common practice for architects to commission a watercolor rendering at that ripe moment when it was time to reveal what a design would look like when built. The perspectivist would labor to make the rendering persuasive, appealing, and sufficiently realistic to inform decisions and sway skeptics. This image would be ceremoniously carried around to client presentations; sometimes an enlarged version would be displayed on the construction fence around the site, like the image in the first chapter. Everyone, even the most naïve viewer, knew this was an imaginative projection, not an image of a building quickly constructed in secret and then photographed.

Linear perspective, graying of background information, selective sharpening or blurring of details, carefully placed humans interacting appropriately—all these were once deployed by perspectivists to draw attention to what was important. Atmospheric perspective, the tendency of elements in the distance to soften and appear slightly blue, is among the more subtle clues to depth. We notice it most in long-distance views, particularly of landscapes. An optical phenomenon, it appears naturally in photographs but not in digital renderings, unless the image-maker intentionally constructs the image *as* an image. (There isn't, at least as far as I know, a "blue it" icon on any digital toolbar.) Depth of field, a technique of differential sharpening and softening, provides that effect in photography, but it is rarely seen in architectural photography. These painterly tropes seem out of place in architectural photography. At least from Ezra Stoller onward, everything in the frame of an architectural photograph manifests equally in focus. Every bone of a Santiago Calatrava building appears equally sharp in one of Alan Karchmer's photographs (Figure 7.3). The focal length for architectural photography is so long that, unless the subject is a detail of a joint or material, depth of field is usually irrelevant. Just set the focal length to infinity and you'll be fine. This is not the case with photography of architectural models, where depth of field has to be carefully disarmed to heighten the illusion that we are looking at the building. That said, the depth of field can be exaggerated to achieve the opposite effect to call ironic attention to its miniatureness.

The perspective in digitally produced renderings is by design flawless, and therefore uncanny. The tool for digital perspective, whether Revit, Rhino, or SketchUp, is a camera and the language used to set up the view is the language of photography—lengths and angles of lenses. Through the camera tool, parallel lines and surfaces converge in the x and y axes changing as the "camera" operator pans and dollies for the best angle. Interestingly, architectural photography regularly employs so-called perspective-correcting lenses to eliminate the undesirable z convergence. Notice in Karchmer's photograph that the sides of the tall surrounding buildings remain parallel into the sky. The weird result is that we have become conditioned to prefer a world where vertical lines and surfaces never converge.

FIGURE 7.3   Photograph of Santiago Calatrava's World Trade Center Transportation Center, opened in 2016, by Alan Karchmer

Yet, this uncanniness isn't solely a function of digital technologies; photography complicates the old certainties. We can detect the uncanny in representations of perspectival space. Consider the image in Figure 7.4 of the Innie Outie House created by virtuoso digital renderer Peter Guthrie, from a design by the firm WOJR. We see in this moody image the by-now-familiar reliance on linear perspective along the x/y axis, but refusal to comply with a vanishing point in the z direction, borrowing the representational conventions of contemporary architectural photography. This is hardly surprising, as Guthrie has a background in architectural

FIGURE 7.4   WOJR's 2012 design for the Innie Outie House, rendered by Peter Guthrie Visualization

photography, and it is an interesting continuation of a circle of influence among painting, photography, and now digital representations. Guthrie, in an interview with *Dezeen* argues that the public is comfortable "reading" architectural renderings. "Most people these days are incredibly familiar with computer-generated images (although they are usually in the form of feature films or computer games) but would find it harder to interpret a line drawing or watercolour of a proposed building."[24] Incredibly familiar...with the unfamiliar. In Guthrie's rendering the viewer is close to the house, standing where only a "familiar" or a trespasser would be. From this position the vertical edges and surfaces should be converging, but they don't because we are in an impossible and yet intimate place. We are looking through the window—should we even be here?—which is reflecting a stone wall behind us, to an empty and minimally furnished bedroom. The unraked leaves, the unfurnished room...what is the story? As arresting as the design is, the image seems to tell a story of abandonment, like the loneliness of masterpiece house-museums where no one lives anymore.

Decades earlier, pre-digital virtuoso Otto Eggers achieved equally uncanny effects in his perspectival drawings for the National Gallery of Art (see Figure 7.5). In this perspective, the scale and distance make the lack of vertical linear convergence less noticeable, but this image is also rectified. Eggers rendered the proposed museum with icy clarity, under a flat grey lightless sky, complying with only two of the three commonly available vanishing points. We are looking south, so there are just a few hints of light—notice the sparkling water of the twin fountains—from what must be a high sun behind the building. A few brave souls approach the building. The trees are in full leaf, casting short shadows, but in the foreground odd fallen leaves lie scattered in the street. Perhaps they fell from the large but unseen tree, which is just out of the frame casting a large shadow on the west corner. What time is it? What season? What planet?

Eggers's drawing would never be confused for a photograph; it is completely atemporal, the very opposite of the camera's captured moment. Eggers's

FIGURE 7.5   Titled simply "National Gallery of Art," this 1936 rendering by Otto Eggers represents the proposed building from the north.

uncanniness is different from Guthrie's, with its painterly fog and photo(un)realistic perspective. It is interesting, though, that both images depict fallen leaves around the buildings. In the real world, fallen leaves on the ground signify both a season and an attitude; they speak of carelessness, abandonment, or maybe a willing concession to nature's invasion into the made world. In the design world, however, those leaves are as carefully constructed and located as every line of the buildings they surround; they are indeed beautifully irrelevant tokens of the uncanny, softening the boundary between reality and imagination.

Architectural renderings are not, then, photographs. Or are they? Visit the website of almost any architecture firm and try to discern among the elegant little project thumbnails which are photographs and which are digital renderings. The very definition of the uncanny lies in this unsettling inability to determine exactly why the thing we're looking at seems both familiar and strange.

Remember Evans's comment quoted earlier about the "figures" that, in the perspective paintings he's discussing, were for the most part imaginary but "based closely on observed studies from life." These people are convincing, he argues, because they *could* be real, because these artists had studied and drawn other humans, all of whom share a fundamental anatomy. Credible humans make imaginary space credible. Architects put people in the their drawings—mostly perspectives, but often in orthographic drawings as well—to signal the relative size of things without recourse to quantitative measure, as well as wordlessly to demonstrate what should happen in a space. A rendering is more than a pleasing image; it is, as we discussed earlier, a rhetorical tool to persuade, provoke, inspire, serve notice, warn, soothe, and rile up all those who see it in preparation for the time-consuming, expensive, irritating, destructive act of fulfillment otherwise known as construction. Inserting images of people just like us, doing the things that we might do, can be vital to the performative function of a perspective rendering.

I would argue that including people in a drawing constitutes a performative—an utterance that does what it says. "I promise" is a performative: by uttering those words, I do indeed make a promise. In architectural renderings, the presence of human figures asserts the reality of the project, its commitment to being constructed. That is their only role because they are not actually part of the project. Like the Tesla in the driveway, they are "not in contract." They can all walk out of the drawing and the imagined building itself will be unchanged, but the imagined *world* will be lost.

J. L. Austin, the philosopher of language, has argued that performatives are neither true nor false, because they aren't assessing reality; they can only be felicitous or infelicitous, happy or unhappy.[25] And what makes a performative happy? A happy performative, Austin argues must meet certain conditions. It must follow a conventional model; you can't simply invent the terms of the promise. Those who make the promise must have the plausible capacity to fulfill it.[26]

A happy performative must be done correctly and completely; finally, the promisers have to be sincere and act in good faith.[27] A thoughtfully populated rendering of a new building is nothing less than the promise of a felicitous new world.

What is Eggers's promise in his drawings for the National Gallery? In the painting galleries (see Figure 7.6) we see dignified figures; all appear to be men in suits, hardly distinguishable as individuals. A few appear slightly translucent—notice how the bench in the foreground passes through the man's topcoat—but that is less a trope, as in contemporary digital renderings, as a function of how the drawing was probably made. None of these gallery-goers is striking

FIGURE 7.6   Eggers's 1936 "Early Study of Exhibition Gallery off Central Gallery" promises a certain kind of experience. And highly polished floors.

a pose, striding purposefully, or betraying any level of art-induced excitement. There is not a single child. They promise that art is serious business, viewed by serious adults. It is revealing to compare Eggers's performatives with those of a contemporary rendering of another art museum in Washington. In drawings of the proposed redesign of the south campus of the Smithsonian Institution, the Bjarke Ingels Group (BIG) portrays people who, like Eggers's people, are gazing at art in a high-ceilinged space (see Figure 7.7). Yet the effect is strikingly different. BIG's people—curiously, mostly women, but also no children—seem deliberately to attract our attention in a way that Eggers's people do not. Why is she wearing sunglasses inside an art gallery? Is it because the space is filled with blinding, white-hot sunlight? Is that why the women are wearing sleeveless dresses? In this newer rendering, we are distracted. We can't help but look at the people *qua* people—who are they?—because we realize that they are not drawn figures but rather images of real people inserted seamlessly into an imaginary world.

Photomontage is an immensely useful rendering technique; but it turns out there are consequences to populating imagined worlds with realistic people. In contemporary renderings, every figure now has a face, a race, a gender, and a mood; the architect has to consider what they're wearing and whether the clothes are appropriate to the setting and the hypothetical season. Above all, despite the blinding light, render people are always happy, even if what they are viewing on the walls of a gallery is not art that would inspire happiness. BIG and Eggers are both making happy performatives, complete and good faith promises, but the BIG rendering has taken us back to the valley. It is not exactly Mori's uncanny valley of creepy robots, but it is uncanny nonetheless.[28]

FIGURE 7.7   Bjarke Ingels Group calls this space the "Art Moat," a new exhibition space planned for the remaking of the Smithsonian's South Campus.

STAIRS

For our last uncanny tell, let's turn our attention to the representation of stairs. In my experience, no architectural element is more confounding for novice architects to draw—more so even than elevations—because stairs serve as the true tests of spatial reasoning and graphicy. What makes stairs such keen diagnostic tools for spatial reasoning? Think about it this way: architects draw plans in layers; a four story building, then, will need at least four plans.[29] Although the plan drawings exist as separate layers—either separate sheets of paper or separate files—there are drawing conventions to signal the material continuity between those layers. The virtual horizontal slicing that separates floors from one another like layers in a cake cuts through walls, partitions, and columns. As we have seen, those cuts may be represented by thicker lines describing the edges of walls, or the insides of walls and columns may be filled in solid, or "*pochéd*." Voids of air such as elevator shafts and plumbing chases also connect one floor to another. And then there are stairs, continuous assemblies of material that rise up through certain specific voids, in seven-inch—the typical rise of a step—increments. Stairs pass through the space in between the sheets of drawings. Picture your four sheets: the stairs begin on one and end on the next, occupying the space between the drawings. A stair drawn correctly in plan will tell the tale of how high above this floor the next floor is, because architects need to know how many steps one needs to get there. Because of their liminal existence, straddling plans with one foot on a lower plan and the other above, they are difficult for beginners to draw accurately and can easily result in M. C. Escher-like uncanny impossibilities.

Thanks to the assistance of computers, stairs can be picked and placed from a digital library of elements with little regard to how they actually ascend and descend between floors. This can have some disconcerting results. J. L. Austin, who has so much to say about doing things with words, talks about the difference between uttering sounds that belong to a vocabulary and uttering sounds in order to mean something, such as reading "a Latin sentence without knowing the meaning of the words."[30] For example, I can utter the sentence "The sign says, '*cave canem*'" without needing to know what "*cave canem*" actually means. Austin refers to this kind of utterance as a "phatic" act, and the Latin bit in this sentence is a "pheme." In uttering this, I am simply quoting a piece of information, which I can convey to another without necessarily understanding it. If, however, I do know what "*cave canem*" means, then I can change my utterance from phatic to rhetic and thus convey meaningful information: "The sign says to beware of the dog." My skill at Latin pronunciation, however, might lead a listener to believe that, even in the phatic utterance, I *do* know what I am saying, and that puts both speaker and listener in a dangerous position, and not only because of the dog.

Phatic utterances are different from gibberish, or a child pretending to write in cursive by making swooping curves along a line. They mean something to someone, but risk being nonsense when they deploy useful things without an understanding of what makes them useful. Phatic stairs—two columns of parallel lines set down in a rectangular space, with a door and its quarter circle swing line at one end—can at first glance appear perfectly competent, located in the correct place, and given plausible space in plan—but they will resist any attempt to extract from them any real information. A rhetic stair—one with a known vocabulary and a commitment to meaning—must indicate its up and down directions, using one or another of the possible conventions, and have a plausible number of treads to make the journey to the next floor, thus telegraphing a third dimension. Some of the phatic difficulties arise from misprecision—precision in the wrong place or at the wrong time in the design process—as when stairs are inserted, CADD-ily, into a drawing where direction hasn't been determined, nor floor-to-floor heights set.

One can avoid the misprecision trap by picking up a pencil and scribbling a few lines to indicate "some kind of stair-like-thing needs to go somewhere around here" which is better than risking a phatic stair before the design is ready. For example, the student drawing in Figure 7.8 shows that hand sketches have a high tolerance for tentativity. There are multiple readings possible for his stair. Are there two parallel possible stairs, their "up" arrows pointing in the same direction? Or are there two stairs divided by the heavy wall? Or are these actually two different optional locations for the stair and its companion wall, sharing the same paper space, like Pope's Donatello Gallery options, to make choosing easier? A closer look

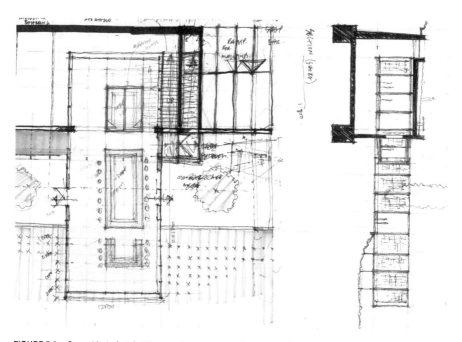

FIGURE 7.8 Some kind of stair thing needs to go somewhere around here.

reveals a lightly drawn penciled stair to the left of the two ink options. Ink in this case signifies slightly more certainty, but the graphite ghost is still there. Nothing has been erased—certainly not deleted—so we can see in the drawing the thinking through of how the stair needs to behave in the building. Notations of tentativity aren't limited to plan drawings. Section sketches with only vague indications of floor-to-floor heights can host "some kind of stair-like-thing" wiggles from one floor to another without premature determinations of numbers of treads or required landings (see Figure 7.9). In these sketches the precision of the drawings is consonant with the precision of the designer; although tentative, these are fully legible rhetic representations of stairs.

Digital drawings seem to carry the greatest phatic risk, resulting in seriously uncanny stairs. The stair in Figure 7.10 is relentlessly accurate and yet completely irrational, deploying a known vocabulary yet without understanding. Try to use it: walk through the door and follow the "up" line; turn at the landing and continue until you slam into the wall right next to where you came in. Because the line weight for the steps themselves is exactly the same as the weight for the line that splits the two runs, it appears that at the end—before you slam into the wall—you can turn left and go up one step and be back where you started. This student has inadvertently drawn a Penrose stair, an impossible object that can only exist in a drawing. There is an "up" arrow indicating direction, but it infelicitously promises only an unrealizable path. The stair in Figure 7.11 offers no clues at all, not even misleading ones, regarding its direction. It dares the viewer to understand it: go ahead, see if you can get anywhere.

It's hard not to conclude that the uncanny is everywhere in architectural drawings: their fundamental responsibility is to combine depictions of what is real—indicative representations—with depictions of what is possible or likely—volitional subjunctive representations. Only when we leave the wishes behind and hone in on the crafting of instructions to build are we making consistently jussive representations of a stable commitment to the real. The uncanny reveals itself in the precision that is out of place and time, and the uncanny accuracy of a digital drawing can act as an unhappy performative. For all too often the rendering is

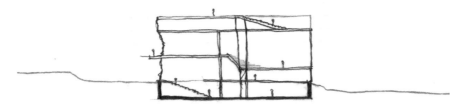

FIGURE 7.9   Two levels will have to be connected somehow, but it's too early to know how.

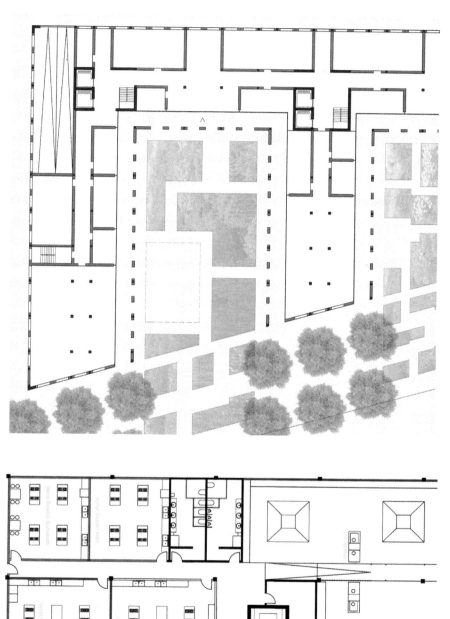

FIGURES 7.10 AND 7.11   Two impossible phatic stairs.

making a promise that the building cannot redeem; that visitors will be happy, that surfaces will be clean and shiny, that the sky will always be cloudless and clear. And the Tesla will be parked in the driveway.

NOTES

1. Sontag, *On Photography*, P 86.
2. Ibid.
3. That sentence is in the subjunctive, expressing a wish contrary to fact, in case you are keeping score.
4. Author Sonit Bafna writes about Mies van der Rohe's iconic drawing of a brick country house and asserts that it cannot really be understood as a possible building because of the incompleteness and inconsistencies of the drawings. It is forever trapped, then, on the design side of the world, in a total eclipse of reality. See Bafna, "How Architectural Drawings Work."
5. This is a comically gross generalization to be sure, but this isn't an art history text. The crisis of representation from the mid-nineteenth century onward was not solely due to the camera; technological, economic, and political developments had been upending the Western world for years already. See Susan Sontag's classic *On Photography* for an image-centric take on this history.
6. Sontag, *On Photography*, P 5.
7. See Karl F. MacDorman and Norri Kageki, translators, "The Uncanny Valley: The Original Essay by Masahiro Mori," *IEEE Spectrum*, June 12, 2012. [https://spectrum.ieee.org/automaton/robotics/humanoids/the-uncanny-valley]
8. Mori, "The Uncanny Valley."
9. Katayama interview, *Wired*, Dec 2011. And the answer is yes, it would be creepy.
10. Mori, "The Uncanny Valley."
11. "Luxo Jr.," about an animated desk lamp, was completed in 1986 and, according to Pixar's website, was the "first three-dimensional animated film to be nominated for an Oscar." See www.pixar.com/our-story-1/#our-story.
12. You will discover how pervasive this view is if you Google "why is the Polar Express movie so creepy?"
13. In *The Pixar Story*, the behind-the-scenes documentary, director Brad Bird somewhat facetiously begins to list the "10 most difficult things to do in animation"; he begins with "humans, hair, fabric, hair and fabric underwater..." He never gets past those four. Humans running is probably on that list.
14. Freud, "The Uncanny," 1919.
15. Ibid.
16. Freud labors for several pages to present this logically, resorting to definitions and derivations from similar words in other languages. His difficulty is itself a lesson in the elusiveness of the uncanny. For an architectural exploration of the concept, see Anthony

Vidler, *The Architectural Uncanny: Essays in the Modern Unhomely*. Our subject here isn't architecture *per se* but its representations so we won't go there.

17. Certain other techniques of drawing and modeling can hold the uncanny in abeyance. By using carefully chosen line weights, selective shadowing, and material suggestions—not for a fully photorealistic rendering, but to tilt toward the real—can productively balance ambiguity and certainty and anchor a drawing in the likely and the possible.

18. Goodman, *Languages of Art*, P 254. Architectural drawings belong to the latter category; *works* of architecture, to the former category.

19. Freud, "The Uncanny," P 15.

20. Funny thing about memory ... I had read this book and the entire trilogy in high school and this scene stuck with me. I was astonished by a description of evil as a subtle violation of the rules of perspective. Or that's how I remembered it, and it remained a vivid image of the disconcerting fragility of the seemingly rational space of the world we inhabit. Oddly, upon rereading for this book, I found less there than I remembered, but it is still enough to evoke the creepiness of the uncanny.

21. Lewis, *The Hideous Strength*, P 297.

22. For more on this see Erwin Panofsky, *Perspective as Symbolic Form*, first published in English in 1927.

23. Evans, *The Projective Cast*, P 138.

24. *Dezeen*, www.dezeen.com/2013/10/20/peterguthrieonhyperrealisticvisualisations/.

25. Austin, *How to do Things with Words*, P 14–15.

26. This is what makes drawings in design competitions unhappy and sometimes dangerous. They are infelicitous performatives; they promise things that the architect has no authority to promise.

27. Ibid.

28. You can buy these people, sometimes called "scalies" or "render people," online, in two and three-dimensional versions. Some are free, but they show up everywhere; if you want unique people you have to pay for them or go hunt and gather them yourself. See this *ArchDaily* post with the inadvertently hilarious title "5 Places to Download Free, Ethnically Diverse Render People," www.archdaily.com/777432/6-websites-for-ethnically-diverse-render-people.

29. I say "at least" because there are such things as reflected ceiling plans and roof plans, which are often necessary depending on the complexity of the project.

30. Austin, *How to do Things with Words*, P 97.

CHAPTER 8
CONCLUSIONS AND QUESTIONS

The contrary secret hidden in all research and design—and design *as* research—is that design doesn't actually solve problems; rather, it raises new ones and exposes previously hidden ones. The good news is that we designers and researchers will never run out of things to do; the bad news is, well, we will never run out of things to do. So it is with this project, which is coming to an end not because I feel as if I have uttered the last word on the subject but because I realize there is no last word. Moreover, perfection is the enemy of the done.

I began this inquiry into how drawings work with confident assertions about the nature and communicative potency of drawings, yet I end with more questions. I have argued, as have others before me, that designers' drawings have different ends than the drawings of artists, even if the means are the same. Their apparent shared languages of representation, however, ultimately split as they establish different relationships to the world. Designers match the world with their drawings, but their ultimate goal is to make the world match the drawings— to change the world. To make that happen, we make sketches, photographs, measured drawings, orthographic projections, perspective projections, diagrams, video, point cloud scans, and models, both digital and physical. Back and forth we go, along the direction-of-fit arrow, drawing from the world as water from a well, to nourish our memories and imaginations for the ongoing task of making and remaking the world. Of that much I am certain. But buried in that list of the stuff we make are media and modes of representation that I have not discussed, even cursorily, and astute readers may already have their own lists of things they think I have irresponsibly ignored.

Now, these questions gather awkwardly in this final chapter, adjacent to some miscellaneous thoughts worth thinking that didn't fit comfortably anywhere else. Hovering above them all is the question of our time, with apologies to Walter Benjamin: what *is* the work of drawing in an age of digital representation and (re) production? To begin to talk about digital drawings, we have to talk about digital models; to talk about digital models, we have to talk about physical models. And so we conclude a book on drawings by talking about models. Are digital and physical models interchangeable? Or are digital models just drawings pretending to be models? What is a "set" of drawings, and why do we need so many different ones? I don't promise to answer these questions—I want to leave something for you to do—but let's at least ask them.

As I mentioned in the preface, I have been chewing on the problematic of representational technologies and graphic communication for a while. By 2004 when I was researching *Tools of the Imagination: Drawing Tools and Technologies from the Eighteenth Century to the Present*, my first exhibition at the National Building Museum[1] (and the project that originally derailed my work on this book), it was clear that the media of design and production, of wishing and instructing, were undergoing a radical transformation. The literature on the subject, however, was more real-time reporting than critical reflecting, so I decided to pick up the phone—such a twentieth-century move—and call a few of the people who were affecting this digital revolution in architectural representation. One of those people was Brad Schell, founder of @Last Software and the creator of SketchUp. In our lengthy conversation, I asked him about the origin of the idea for SketchUp, and how he would describe his groundbreaking software.

Schell, an engineer by training, had worked for a concrete pre-cast company designing formwork, which he described as a "giant 3D jigsaw puzzle."[2] He quickly realized that operating in a 3D virtual environment was more challenging for some than for others, and wondered if there wasn't a better way to do things. Schell had already developed one 3D program, the charmingly named CADzooks, which he sold to Autodesk in 1996. In 2000 he and his co-developer Joe Esch released SketchUp with the mission "to make 3D accessible to almost anybody—kids, elderly, gamers, woodworkers..." Although it may look like one and act like one, SketchUp, Schell explained, was not a modelling program. Instead, it is a three-dimensional *drawing* program, a "magical blank sheet and pen" that "captures the spirit of drawing."[3] Its only tools are tools of drawing: virtual pencils and erasers, and little icons of drawing types. It has no virtual warehouse or "library" stocked with architectural elements, like columns, walls, or even Penrose stairs. Like Harold with his purple crayon, a SketchUp user simply draws in the air, or whatever ethereal substance constitutes the CADmosphere.[4]

True digital modelling programs differ from SketchUp's air-drawing in significant ways, not the least of which rests on the difference between a drawing and a model. Drawing is, in the words of technology scholar Carl Mitcham, "a kind of testing of interrelating of various factors by miniature building."[5] How much more effective and predictive might that testing be if the miniature building were in fact a miniature building? Architects have always constructed miniature buildings; traditionally they were simply called "models." Digital technologies have problematized that word. It can't travel alone anymore; the word "model" needs to be chaperoned by one of its modifiers, "digital" or "physical," lest it be misunderstood. If SketchUp's 3D drawings aren't models, then what *is* a digital model? And what is it not? It is a miniature building, but its miniatureness isn't stable, because it has no fixed scale. It is itself amaterial—virtual—but it denotes and can depict real material. A digital model presents itself as if three-dimensional, but only as seen through the looking glass of the computer screen. It can't be touched, smelled, or dropped on the floor, without massive collateral damage to the computer that hosts it.

Most digital models that architects make today are Building Information Models (BIM), the development of which is arguably the most radical disruption in architectural representation and practice since the photochemical process of blueprinting allowed the separation of the instructions for a building from its construction site, and thus the architect from the builders.[6] According to the National Building Information Model Standard Project Committee, a Building Information Model is

> a digital representation of physical and functional characteristics of a facility. A BIM is a shared knowledge resource for information about a facility forming a reliable basis for decisions during its life-cycle; defined as existing from earliest conception to demolition.[7]

From "conception to demolition," a building can now have a virtual avatar for its entire life, recording its milestones of construction, space planning, addition, and renovation. (What happens at demolition? Does the BIM self-destruct?) BIM is, as the name promises, a model of information in which each element comes loaded with the properties of its real-world compliants; in that respect, it comes closer to Mitcham's predictive miniature building than any other form of drawing or model. Constructed of instantiations of architectural elements, the BIM doesn't simply look like the building; it is a virtual version of the building, not a depiction, but a high-definition denotation.

A BIM isn't a drawing, although every type of architectural drawing—plans, sections, elevations, axonometrics, perspectives, and more—can be extracted from it. In the same way that magnetic resonance imaging (MRI) produces innumerable slices through the three-dimensional body to describe changes, a series of relentlessly accurate sections can be sliced through a building information model. A year's worth of sunrises and sunsets can be mapped across the BIM, in minute-by-minute increments if so desired. Such a quantity of information can provoke the numbness of TMI—too much information—as well as the blindness of TIA—technology-induced amnesia, a condition where powerful tools leave us bereft of common knowledge and commoner sense.[8] The difficult questions this information saturation provokes take us back to Stinchcombe's concept of cognitive economy and cognitive sufficiency: what do we really need to represent in our miniature buildings, and to whom?[9]

What about physical models? How do they differ from the digital, aside from the obvious? (see earlier comments about touch, smell, and dropping on floors) One of my early mentors in practice shared his rule for presenting design ideas in client meetings: keep the model hidden until you've walked them through the drawings. If they see the model first, he warned, you'll never get them to pay attention to the drawings. A physical model, a miniature building, is simply too compelling an object, bleaching the life out of everything around it (see Figure 8.1). Although they share the same noun, physical models are doomed never to meet their digital cousins in real space. Whereas the power of digital models resides in their point-for-point correspondence to the anticipated building—represented in the epiphenomena of the image, like the underlying code in *The Matrix*—the power of physical models comes from an entirely different source, what we might irreverently call the transubstantiation of cardboard. The elements in a digital model originate as instantiations for elements in the real world, adhering to Mitchell's "triangular pattern of reference" that we mentioned earlier.[10] For example, the natural language name "concrete wall" corresponds to an information-supported representation of a concrete wall, which in turn anticipates the one to be built. In a BIM, this concrete wall has specificity and dimension. Physical model parts, on the other hand, come not only from fresh foam core and chipboard, but from discarded boxes, wood scraps, window screen, even parts cannibalized from other

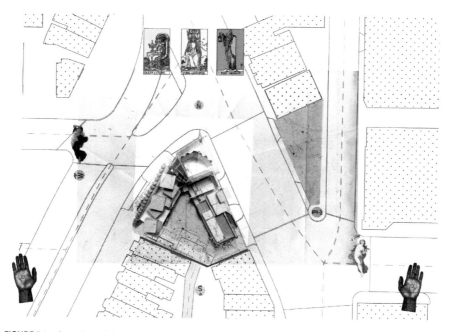

FIGURE 8.1   A study model under construction atop a base drawing, which already looks pale by comparison. By Abi Kallushi

models. Only through the act of *making* the model do these extra-architectural materials acquire architectural intentions and begin to point toward possible materials in the real world (see Figure 8.2). In the hands and imagination of the architect, cardboard receives what John Searle calls "propositional content."[11] Searle asks, "How does the mind impose Intentionality on entities that are not intrinsically Intentional, on entities such as sounds and marks that are, construed in one way, just physical phenomena in the world like any other?"[12] In other words, if I say this drinking straw is a column, then this drinking straw *is* a column.

Cardboard is among the most banal species of material in the world; its ultimate fate is usually the recycling bin. Yet it has a remarkable expressive range: when laid flat and cut along the curvilinear contours of the topographic lines of a landscape, it represents earth (see Figure 8.3); cut into strips and stacked, it represents masonry; deployed vertically in sheets and given a certain thickness or marked in a certain way, it intends toward concrete (see Figure 8.4). The slight but constant uncertainty of what the cardboard intends in ambiguous applications is in fact essential to the design process, the three-dimensional equivalent of a hand-drawn sketch; they are physical subjunctive wishes. The architect pours a measure of intentionality into the physical model but then the client adds her own dose of impressions and creative misreadings. In this way, the model can also speak in the consultative register and it then remains an open work, most useful

FIGURE 8.2 Anything at hand can be imbued with architectural intent by the model-maker. By Abi Kallushi

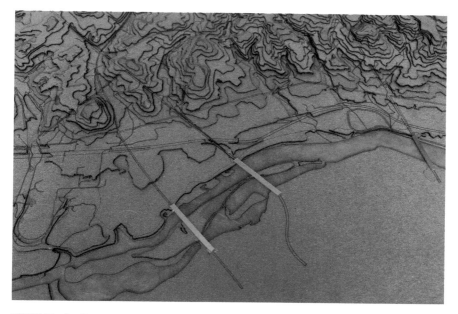

FIGURE 8.3   Cardboard becomes earth in this student model of the topography east of the Anacostia River.

FIGURE 8.4   Different model materials intend toward, but do not literally represent, possible real materials.
By Dan Snook

and appropriate to the wishing phase. The BIM is capable of wishing—albeit in its inescapably precise way—but it fulfills its true mission by instructing.

What about efforts to make full-size models, either digital or physical? Why are we still stuck in miniatures? There have been efforts, both low-tech and hi-tech, to bypass drawings and models and instead allow people to experience immersive simulations of architectural proposals. Switzerland for example, requires that the total extent of a proposed project be staked on its site prior to receiving a building permit so that affected parties can see at least the outline of the building-to-come.[13] Also in the Swiss study discussed earlier, the Laboratory for Architectural Experimentation (LEA) at the Ecole Polytechnique Federale de Lausanne launched a research project to see if people could make better decisions about a future project if they could use blocks to build full-scale models of parts of buildings.[14] In this case, the subject population was composed of future residents of a housing project, and the scale of interaction was limited to one's own unit. Leaving aside the limits of *physically* modeling a building at full scale, the LEA study suffered from the same shortcoming as immersive digital simulations: only the space is modeled, not the material stuff. The participants at the LEA were given a set of modular white plastic blocks with which to build, with the result communicating little of the experience of place. The result was more akin to a giant foam-core or LEGO brick model than a miniature building. The amateriality of such an experiment only serves inadvertently to reify the suspicion that modern architecture is an abstraction, withdrawn from the world of gravity, grout, and splinters. We are still a long way from the Holodeck on the Enterprise, that dream of haptic simulation (just don't forget the safety protocols), even when experiences such as this are done with augmented or virtual reality equipment. None of these yet equal the communicative richness and informational density of a drawing, even a dangerous elevation. But they can give you motion sickness.

Instructions to build, as we discussed in Chapter 5, require more than a single drawing unless that building is a snap-together garden shed. Any building of even modest complexity requires a *set* of drawings—even though BIM challenges this too—the discussion of which gives us the opportunity to explore one last obscure corner of the subjunctive. In Chapter 3, I explained the different verb modes and mentioned that the subjunctive mode—an expressive leap forward from just naming and ordering others around—"yoked" previously independent clauses together to form more complex molecules of meaning in coordinate and subordinate clauses. Another way of describing those coordinate and subordinate clauses—as if we need another way—is as "paratactic" and "hypotactic" sequences.

"Parataxis" is the placement of things side by side without connecting elements or conjunctions; they are joined by proximity or, perhaps in the case of the set of drawings, by convention.[15] My desk, for example, has a paratactic stack of drawings on it—an unfiltered, random heap of possible selections I considered for inclusion in this book. The final selection, though, forms a hypotactic set: drawings linked with conjunctions/connections embedded in the content of these chapters. It is through coordination and conjunction that a *group* of drawings becomes a *set*.

Architectural drawings, particularly in the instruction/construction phase, constitute hypotactic sets in which types of drawings appear in a customary sequence tied to scales and categories of information. From the opening drawings of location, plat plan, and site plan, we begin to zoom in to the building plans, then conceptually lift our eyes to the section and elevations, and finally continue to zoom to details. The set makes space for the drawings of the other disciplines necessary for contemporary construction, again in an expected sequence that includes structural, plumbing, mechanical, electrical and more, depending on building type. In that sense, sets of drawings, even in the era of BIM, communicate in their own frozen register and have conventions of navigation to guide the viewer from the general to the specific, down a detail trail only to return to the next floor plan to continue the journey. No single drawing is cognitively sufficient to contain the totality of the instructions.

We have spent the last several thousand words talking about what architectural drawings are and how they work; it's also worth remembering what architectural drawings aren't. They are both more and other than graphics, and are not to be evaluated—although they may be enjoyed—according their trendiness, cleverness, coolness, or the ways in which seductive geometric complexities play across their two-dimensional surfaces. Nor are they art, although there is an art to them. Their value as art, when they occasionally slip out of their architectural roles and into the shifting currents of the art market, derives from attributes external to their value as living, breathing, wishing and instructing documents, with specific illocutionary force. Such is the curious fate of Otto Eggers's drawings of the West Building; deemed more "art" than architecture—as we mentioned earlier—they are housed in the Modern Prints and Drawings Collection, rather than in the Gallery's Archives. They have been removed from the *set* of drawings, the wishes and instructions, for the 1939 building (see Figure 8.5) and their formal and technical mastery has eclipsed their original role as deontic drawings—wishes directed toward action. More beautiful than useful, they are no longer living drawings in an ongoing conversation with the building they wished into existence. They have become history.

Architecture's alliance with art has not helped its quest for professional legitimacy or cultural necessity; it perpetuates the mystification of the field and the perception of it as a luxury. On the one hand, the rarefied quality of Eggers's drawings only serves to reinforce these marginalizations. On the other hand, what an honor is being bestowed on Otto Eggers by the recognition that his hand is not just the executor of utilitarian instructions and expedient descriptions. He has drawn a world that is fully habitable in the imagination, with or without the building.

Architectural drawings are also not personal—you can't make up your own graphic conventions and signifiers any more than you can make up a personal language, unless your goal is to isolate yourself from others. To participate in the gregarious enterprise of world-making you must consent to a shared—but by no means static—grammar. Even the most personally expressive drawings (see Figure 8.6) are grounded in known languages. If you have the pleasure of spending a short time with a set of hand-drawn drawings, as I have with my students', as well as

FIGURE 8.5   This curious drawing, titled "View from the Rotunda Ceiling to Floor Below: Five Black Columns Showing," is a partial axonometric, a three-dimensional projection capable of showing material on adjacent surfaces, something difficult to show in a physical model.

FIGURE 8.6   Abi Kallushi

I.M. Pei's and Otto Eggers's, you will appreciate the hands and minds that crafted them. The drawings for the East Building are by no means antiques and while there's very little material nostalgia attached to plastic lead and Mylar, they have a strange archaic quality now, in the time of BIM. It may be my imagination—the sign of excellent drawings is their power to provoke imagination, after all—but in the quiet hours I spent looking over them in the archives of the National Gallery, I began to feel the team effort, the myriad hands that wrote these notes, cut the Pantone, and drew these details. If I were to turn my attention to such arcana, I could probably discern the different hands in the rendering of materials and even the lettering; everyone who worked on these drawings stippled, hatched, and outlined slightly differently. In the lettering, I can almost tell when a deadline is approaching; in this way, time and urgency are carried in the marks on Mylar, as is certainty and tentativity. Digital drawings and their supplemental notes never give up the identities of their authors, as if to protect the innocent.

Digital models fulfill the architect's dream for a drawing that can spin around in space, revealing all sides of the building in any view desired, and one we can alter directly, rather than having to make a change in plan then follow its consequences through the entire set to make sure that the change appears in all the necessary drawings. The promise of BIM is one-step coordination. Whether "on" the drawing board or "in" the computer, the architect makes a new world in which to act. The preposition flip is interesting: "on" paper, "on" the drawing board, but "in" the computer. The drawing on paper occupies a space, a surface analogous to the site itself, a place on which a building or place emerges. Paper is ground. The computer is a box—and a black box at that, no matter its actual color or finish—and we talk about putting information *into* it, even as we talk about what is *on* the screen, as if the screen reveals just the epiphenomena of the machinations inside.

Digital production of architectural drawings is pushing the specificity trajectory further upstream in the design process, icing creative ambiguities and tentativities earlier in the design process and increasing the risks of misprecision. As linguists have feared that English has lost the subjunctive, and with it a capacity to express certain things, are we losing the subjunctive in drawing? Is the only remaining distinguishing mark of subjunctivity the file extension "_draft"? Is that all we have to know through which lens of tentativity to read the information?

Is that how drawings work now? Do they work differently now that they have left the paper on the table and migrated to the virtual air behind the screen? If the goal of drawing—from the world and to the world—has always been to squish the three-dimensional world onto a two-dimensional surface, do Sketch-Up's air-drawing of wishes and laser scanning's world-matching point clouds represent the apotheosis of drawing, or its end? Are drawings ready to retire after thousands of years of work and hand off all the world-matching and world-making responsibilities to our new virtual assistants? What is a drawing, really? With apologies to Victor Hugo, will this kill that?

NOTES

1. The eponymous companion book is still available, in case you want to read more about the technology side of drawing.
2. This comes from my handwritten notes from a 2004 phone conversation with Schell.
3. Schell joked that this was one reason that "all the old guys" in architecture liked SketchUp. Its interface built on a skill they already had: drawing.
4. It is telling that where SketchUp has an eraser icon to delete lines and elements from its air-drawing, Revit, the dominant BIM program, has a hammer to "demolish" elements in the model, as if they are "real."
5. Mitcham, *Thinking Through Technology*, P 224.
6. It is difficult today to imagine the radical changes brought about simply by the ability to make multiple accurate copies from a single original drawing. We press "print" today as many times as we like, rarely pondering the weirdness of the sudden extinction of the species known as original drawings. Or are they all originals?
7. For a practice-changing technology such as BIM, it was inevitable that a formal structure and standards were necessary:

   > A structure is needed in order to scope the inter-relationship of projects as well as define the overall range of projects to define a Building Information Model. Without such a structure, there is no end to the effort and no understanding of what we are collectively developing.

   See www.nationalbimstandard.org/tetralogyofbim for a front-row seat to watch the evolution of a Stinchcombian formal system in real time.
8. TIA is a common affliction—you suffer from it if you can no longer remember your mother's phone number, how to do long division, or how your grandmother kept the house cool without air-conditioning.
9. In his tome *The Information: A History, a Theory, a Flood*, James Gleick explains, "What makes cyberspace different from all previous information technologies is its intermixing of scales from the largest to the smallest without prejudice..." P 77.
10. Mitchell, *The Logic of Architecture*, P 64.
11. Searle, *Intentionality: An Essay in the Philosophy of Mind*, P 5.
12. Ibid, P 27.
13. www.locationswitzerland.com/internet/osec/en/home/invest/us/handbook/real_estate/building_permits.html.
14. Lawrence, "Laypeople as Architectural Designers."
15. While paratactic sequences are linguistically less sophisticated than hypotactic ones, this is not to say that parataxis doesn't generate its own peculiar poetry, such as the familiar surrealist activity of collective creativity, the exquisite corpse. For those with interest and too much time, there are several exquisite corpse websites; see the Exquisite Corpse Server at http://bluestem.hort.purdue.edu/ecs/.

BIBLIOGRAPHY

Ackerman, James. *Origins, Imitation, Conventions: Representations in the Visual Arts*. Cambridge, MA: The MIT Press, 2002

Aristotle, *Rhetoric*. Trans. W. Rhy Roberts, http://classics.mit.edu/Aristotle/rhetoric.mb.txt

_____. *Poetics*. Trans. Malcolm Heath. New York: Penguin Classics, 1996

Austin, J.L. *How to do Things with Words*. Ed. J.O. Urmson and Marina Sbisà. 2d ed. Cambridge, MA: Harvard University Press, 1975

Bachelard, Gaston. *The Poetics of Space*. Boston: Beacon Press, 1969

Bafna, Sonit. 2008. "How Architectural Drawings Work—and What That Implies for the Role of Representation in Architecture." *The Journal of Architecture* 13:5, 535–564

Barthes, Roland. *Image, Music, Text*. New York: Hill and Wang, 1977

Berk, Lynn M. *English Syntax: From Word to Discourse*. New York: Oxford University Press, 1999

Benjamin, Walter. "The Work of Art in the Age of Mechanical Reproduction." *Illuminations*. New York: Harcourt Brace, 1968

Boyd, Julian and J.P. Thorne. 1969. "The Semantics of Modal Verbs." *The Journal of Linguistics* 5, 57–74

Bronowski, Jacob. *The Origins of Knowledge and Imagination*. New Haven, CT: Yale University, 1978

Calvino, Italo. *Invisible Cities*. New York: Harcourt, Inc., 1972

Chomsky, Noam. *Aspects of the Theory of Syntax*. Cambridge, MA: The MIT Press, 1965

Cosgrove, Denis, ed. *Mappings*. London: Reaktion Books, Ltd., 1999

Cuff, Dana. *Architecture: The Story of Practice*. Cambridge, MA: The MIT Press, 1991

Emmons, Paul. 1998. "The Cosmogony of Bubble Diagrams." 86th ACSA Annual Meeting Proceedings, Constructing Identity, 420–425

Evans, Robin. *Translations from Drawing to Building and Other Essays*. Cambridge, MA: The MIT Press, 1997

_____. *The Projective Cast: Architecture and its Three Geometries*. Cambridge, MA: The MIT Press, 2000

Filarete. *Treatise on Architecture*. Trans. John R. Spencer. New Haven, CT: Yale University Press, 1965

Frascari, Marco. "The Tell-the-Tale Detail." *Semiotics 1981*. Eds. John N. Deely, Morgot D Lenhart. New York, NY: Plenum Press, 1980

Freud, Sigmund. *The Uncanny*. Trans. Alix Strachey. First published in Imago, Bd. V., 1919, Funfte Folge

Gardner, Howard. *Frames of Mind: The Theory of Multiple Intelligences*. New York: Basic Books, 1983

Gleick, James. *The Information: A History, a Theory, a Flood*. New York: Pantheon Books, 2011

Goodman, Nelson. *Ways of World Making*. Indianapolis, IN: Hackett Publishing, 1978

_____. *Languages of Art: An Approach to a Theory of Symbols*. New York: Bobbs-Merrill Company, 1968

Greenough, Horatio. *Form and Function: Remarks on Art, Design, and Architecture*. Ed. Harold A. Small. Los Angeles: University of California Press, 1947

Grice, Paul. *Studies in the Way of Words*. Cambridge, MA: Harvard University Press, 1989

Gruzdyz, Sophia. January 2002. "Drawing: The Creative Link." *Architectural Record*, 190:1, 64

Harsh, Wayne. *The Subjunctive in English*. Birmingham: University of Alabama Press, 1968

Hricak, Michael, FAIA, ed. *The Architecture Student's Handbook of Professional Practice*. 14th ed. Hoboken, NJ: John Wiley and Sons, 2009

Illich, Ivan. *Tools for Conviviality*. New York: Harper & Row, 1973

Jakobson, Roman. "Closing Statement: Linguistics and Poetics." *Style in Language*. Ed. Thomas Sebeok. Cambridge MA: MIT Press, 1960. 350–377

James, Francis. *Semantics of the English Subjunctive*. Vancouver: University of British Columbia Press, 1986

Johnson, Crockett. *Harold and the Purple Crayon*. New York: Harper Collins, 1955

Joos, Martin. *The Five Clocks*. New York: Harcourt, Brace & World, Inc., 1967

Klein, Robert. *Form and Meaning: Essays on the Renaissance and Modern Art*. Trans. Madeline Jay and Leon Wieseltier. New York: Viking Press, 1970

Langer, Suzanne K. *Feeling and Form*. New York: Charles Scribner's Sons. 1955

Lawrence, Roderick T. Summer 1983. "Laypeople as Architectural Designers." *Leonardo*, 16:3, *Special Issue: Psychology and the Arts*. Cambridge, MA: MIT Press, 232–236

Lewis, C. S. *The Hideous Strength*. New York: Macmillan, 1967

Lewis, David. *Counterfactuals*. Malden, MA: Blackwell Publishers, 1971

Mitcham, Carl. *Thinking through Technology: The Path between Engineering and Philosophy*. Chicago, IL: University of Chicago Press, 1994

Mitchell, William J. *The Logic of Architecture: Design, Computation, and Cognition*. Cambridge, MA: The MIT Press, 1990

Mori, Masahiro. 1970. "The Uncanny Valley." Trans. Karl F. MacDorman and Takashi Minato. *Energy* 7:4, 33–35

Peirce, Charles S. *The Essential Writings*. Ed. Edward C. Moore. Amherst NY: Prometheus Books, 1998

Piedmont-Palladino, Susan C. *Tools of the Imagination: Drawing Tools and Technologies from the Eighteenth Century to the Present*. New York: Princeton Architectural Press, 2007

Pliny. *Natural History IX, Libri XXXIII–XXXV*. Trans. H. Rackham. Cambridge, MA: Harvard University Press, 1961

Quinn, Arthur. *Figures of Speech: 60 Ways to Turn a Phrase*. Layton, UT: Gibbs M. Smith, Inc., 1982

Richards, I.A. and C.S. Lewis. *The Philosophy of Rhetoric*. Oxford: Oxford University Press, 1936

Ricoeur, Paul. *Interpretation Theory: Discourse and the Surplus of Meaning*. Fort Worth: Texas Christian University, 1976

_____. *The Rule of Metaphor: Multi-Disciplinary Studies in the Creation of Meaning*. Trans. Robert Czerny, with Kathleen McLaughlin and John Costello, 1977. Toronto: University of Toronto Press, reprint 2008

_____. June 1979. "The Function of Fiction in Shaping Reality." *Man and World*, 12:2, 123–141

Robbins, Edward. *Why Architects Draw*. Cambridge, MA: The MIT Press, 1994

Ryle, Gilbert. *The Concept of Mind.* New York: Barnes and Noble, 1949

Scheer, Brenda Case and Wolfgang F.E. Preiser, eds. *Design Review: Challenging Urban Aesthetic Control.* New York: Chapman and Hall, 1994

Schön, Donald. *The Reflective Practitioner: How Professionals Think in Action.* New York: Basic Books, 1983

Searle, John. *Intentionality: An Essay in the Philosophy of Mind.* New York: Cambridge University Press, 1983

Sennett, Richard. *The Craftsman.* New Haven, CT: Yale University Press, 2008

Sontag, Susan. *On Photography.* New York: Anchor Books, 1977

Stinchcombe Arthur L., *When Formality Works: Authority and Abstraction in Law and Organizations,* Chicago IL: The University of Chicago Press, 2001

Tartre, Lindsay Anne. May 1990. "Spatial Orientation Skill and Mathematical Problem Solving." *Journal for Research in Mathematics Education,* 21:3, 216–229

Ventola, Eija, ed. *Discourse and Community: Doing Functional Linguistics.* Tubingen: Gunter Narr Verlag Tubingen., 2000

Walton, Kendall. *Mimesis as Make-Believe: On the Foundations of the Representational Arts.* Cambridge, MA: Harvard University Press, 1990

White, Alan R. *The Language of Imagination.* Cambridge MA: Basil Blackwell, 1990

Yates, Frances A. *The Art of Memory.* Chicago IL: The University of Chicago Press, 1974

Zumthor, Peter. *Thinking Architecture.* Baden, Germany: Lars Mueller, 1988

PERIODICALS

The Washington Post, 18 October 2016, "The 'Higgs Bison' Mystery Is Solved with the Help of Ancient Cave Paintings," author: Sara Kaplan

Federal Register, 19 September 1983, "HABS/HAER Standards: Secretary of the Interior's Standards and Guidelines for Architectural and Engineering Documentation," Washington, DC

Nature Communications, 18 October 2016, "Early Cave Art and Ancient DNA Record the Origin of the European Bison," authors: Julien Soubrier, Graham Gower, et al.

Popular Science, October 2011, 279:4, "Scientist in a Strange Land," author: Tom Clyne

Proceedings of the National Academy of Sciences, 7 November 2011, 108:46, "Genotypes of Predomestic Horses Match Phenotypes Painted in Paleolithic Works of Cave Art," authors: Melanie Pruvost, Rebecca Bellone, et al.

WEB SOURCES

Dezeen: accessed February 2016 www.dezeen.com/2013/08/12/henrygossonarchitecturalvisualisations/

Dezeen: accessed February 2016 www.dezeen.com/2013/10/20/peterguthrieonhyperrealisticvisualisations/

Katayama, Lisa, Interview with Masahito Mori, Dec 2011 www.wired.com/magazine/2011/11/pl_mori/

IMAGE CREDITS

PREFACE

CHAPTER 1

CHAPTER 2

CHAPTER 3

CHAPTER 4

CHAPTER 5

CHAPTER 6

CHAPTER 7

CHAPTER 8

INDEX

Note: Page numbers in *italics* refer to figures.

uncanny valley 140–142
understanding through drawing 87–91
units of architectural meaning 33–37

Van Eyck, Jan 6–7
verbs 54–58; modes and architectural
    drawings 58–60
Villa Gamberaia 87–88, *89–90*
volitional expressions 4, 52, 57, 95–104

wishes 51–53; and instructions 130–131,
    154–155; for National Gallery East Building
    94–104; overlap between instruction
    phase and 138–139; physical models and
    162–163
WOJR 147, *147*
Woods, Lebbeus 31

Zumthor, Peter 25, 29, 87